Serena Williams

Biography of Her Life, Career & History

(Queen of the Court Bids the Tennis World Farewell)

Jennifer Weizzz

Published By **Chris David**

Jennifer Weizzz

All Rights Reserved

Serena Williams: Biography of Her Life, Career & History (Queen of the Court Bids the Tennis World Farewell)

ISBN 978-1-77485-891-2

No part of this guidebook shall be reproduced in any form without permission in writing from the publisher except in the case of brief quotations embodied in critical articles or reviews.

Legal & Disclaimer

The information contained in this ebook is not designed to replace or take the place of any form of medicine or professional medical advice. The information in this ebook has been provided for educational & entertainment purposes only.

The information contained in this book has been compiled from sources deemed reliable, and it is accurate to the best of the Author's knowledge; however, the Author cannot guarantee its accuracy and validity and cannot be held liable for any errors or omissions. Changes are periodically made to this book. You must consult your doctor or get professional medical advice before using any of the suggested remedies, techniques, or information in this book.

Upon using the information contained in this book, you agree to hold harmless the Author from and against any damages, costs, and expenses, including any legal fees potentially resulting from the application of any of the information provided by this guide. This disclaimer applies to any damages or injury caused by the use and application, whether directly or indirectly, of any advice or information presented, whether for breach of contract, tort, negligence, personal injury, criminal intent, or under any other cause of action.

You agree to accept all risks of using the information presented inside this book. You need to consult a professional medical practitioner in order to ensure you are both able and healthy enough to participate in this program.

TABLE OF CONTENTS

Chapter 1: Childhood Life 1

Chapter 2: Family 8

Chapter 3: Journey To Success 15

Chapter 4: Match Controversies...100

Chapter 5: Dateting Historization .112

Chapter 6: 20 Outstanding Secrets About Serena Williams 119

Chapter 7: Serena's Most Popular Rivals 131

Chapter 8: The Legacy Of Serena Williams..153

Chapter 9: Serana Retirement 162

Chapter 1: Childhood Life

Serena Jameka Williams is an American tennis player born on the 26th of September 1981.

Serena was born the 26th of September 1981 in the home of Oracene Price and Richard Williams in Saginaw, Michigan. She is the eldest of Price's five children which includes her full-grown younger sister Venus as well as half sisters Yetunde, Lyndrea, and Isha Price.

In addition she has at the very least seven half-siblings from her paternal side. She started play tennis as a child at four when the family moved into Compton, California when the children were very young.

Serena Williams' parents, Oracene Price and Richard Williams, also taught her younger sister Venus.

Williams along with her entire family moved her family to West Palm Beach, Florida at the age of nine older, so she could take part in Rick Macci's tennis academy that offered her additional coaching. Macci was pleased that Williams her father "treated his children as if they were kids and let them be girls" although he was not always with him.

Williams was aged 10 when Richard had stopped taking his girls to national junior tennis tournaments due to his desire to "progress at a slower pace" and focus on their studies. The decision was also influenced by his experiences with racism, as he witnessed white parents mocking the Williams sisters while they competed.

Williams was rated the top among the under-10 players of Florida at the time , and was a 46-3 winner in his United States Tennis Association junior tour.

She made the transition to professional tennis in 1995. The US Open in 1999 saw her take the first significant singles win. The American was undefeated from 2002's French Open through the 2003 Australian Open, winning all four major singles titles (each time beating Venus at the end of each final) and then completing her record-breaking career Grand Slam, often known as the "Serena Slam."

She also won two singles championships over the next many years, however, she also suffered injuries and a decrease in her performance. However, beginning in 2007 she slowly recovered her fitness, despite persistent illness, and was able to regain her spot at the top of the world singles rankings.

Williams has regained her dominance with her participation in the Wimbledon Championships in 2012, winning the Olympic gold medal and being the only tennis athlete to achieve the Career Golden Slam in both doubles and singles. She was able to complete her third "Serena Slam" by winning eight of the 13 singles majors, which included the four consecutive majors between 2014 and 2015. She set Steffi Graf's Open Era record by winning her 23rd major singles tournament at 2017. She won her 23rd major singles championship at the Australian Open. Then, she took a sabbatical from tennis professionalism following the discovery that she was pregnant after which, since she began playing again she has progressed up to 4 major championships.

Along together with sibling Venus, Williams won 14 major women's doubles championships winning without a loss at Grand Slam doubles finals. This includes the Grand Slam that took place outside of the calendar year in between 2010's Wimbledon Championships and the 2010 French Open, which gave the sisters the number. #1 doubles ranking around the globe. Her sister holds the record for highest number of Olympic gold medals with four. Three of them were won by women's doubles. She also took home two major mixed doubles championships in 1998. Williams told the tennis world about her plans to retire in August 2022.

One of the greatest tennis players ever is generally thought of as Williams. A new age of strength and athleticism on the women's professional tennis circuit is connected to Williams' entry. Williams sisters' participation.

With 39 major titles to her name in doubles, singles and mixed doubles--23 for singles and 14 in women's doubles and two mixed doubles -- Serena has the highest number of active players. When it comes to total major titles she has she has won, she is second for her age group in the Open Era and tied for third overall.

Williams was asked in 2000 whether it would be more beneficial for them to have been following the standard routine of playing regularly on the junior circuit "Everybody does things differently. Venus and I could have just tried an alternative route, and it worked in our case."

Most recently, a woman has managed to be awarded the Surface Slam (major championships on clay, hard, and grass courts during the exact same year) It was her turn in the year 2015. She's also the first woman to hold the major singles titles of all four (2002-03 as well as 2014 to 2015). Alongside Venus She is also the first player holding all of the women's doubles titles at the same time (2009-10).

Williams was paid around $29.9 million during 2016, which makes her the most highly-paid female athlete in the world. With $27 million of cash prizes as well as sponsorships. She matched the record in 2017, when she was the sole female to be named on Forbes' list of top 100 most-paid athletes. In addition , to being named Sportsperson of the Year by Sports Illustrated magazine in December 2015, she's won this Laureus Sportswoman of the Year award four times (in 2003 in

2003, 2010, 2016 and in 2018). She was ranked as the 28th spot according to Forbes's list of most highly paid athletes in the world as of 2021. She is the most-paid female athlete.

Chapter 2: Family

RICHARD WILLIAMS The FATHER

The place he was raised is Shreveport, Louisiana, on February 16 1942. He moved first to Chicago after completing high school, before making his final destination California. When he was in the year 1965, he married Betty Johnson for the first time, but they split in 1973. Together, they have three sons and three daughters.

He then got married Oracene Price on the 29th of September, 1979, and gave birth to Serena and Venus the younger sister of Serena. Their marriage was not finalized till Venus had her first child. The couple divorced in 2002. filed for divorced citing irreconcilable differences for the cause.

He married Lakeisha Graham in 2010 she is one years older than his daughter Venus. In 2012 the couple welcomed a new son along with Lakeisha. He also released "Black and White The Perspective I Take." He suffered a stroke two years after the publication However, he's reported to be doing better now.

ORACENE PRICE The Mother

Oracene Price, formerly known also as Brandy Price, was born on the 3rd of April 1952 at Saginaw, Michigan. Prior to pursuing a education at Western Michigan University, she went to Buena Vista High School, where she completed her studies and graduated in the year 1970. Prior to her death she got engaged with Yusef Rasheed.

The mother of her children, Yetunde Price Lyndrea Price and Isha Price through their union.

Then, she got married to Richard Williams, the father of Venus and Serena who are her children. She and Richard changed their ways in 2000 and divorced on a legal basis in 2002. After divorce, she reverted to the name she had used as her first.

THE SISTERS WILLIAMS

When they were 3 years old, the father started making preparations for Serena and her older sister Venus for a career in tennis. Venus and Serena transformed the way their sport was viewed due to their unique style of play and performances. They dominated their opponents due to their strength and athleticism Their presence and flair earned them fame on the court.

The close-knit group of sisters lived in the same home in Florida's exclusive Palm Beach Gardens community for more than a decade however, they split up after Serena bought a house in the nearby town of Jupiter in December 2013.

When Serena was the winner of in the U.S. Open in 1999 She beat the Williams sister Venus in the race to win the first time in their family's history to win a Grand Slam victory. This set the stage that allowed the two Williams sisters to win numerous notable victories.

Serena and Venus joined forces in 2008 to earn another Olympic gold medal in women's doubles at the Beijing Games. In 2009, Serena and Venus became the first African American women to buy an interest of an NFL franchise when they purchased shares of the Miami Dolphins.

At the doubles women's tournament in the 2012 Summer Olympics, Serena and her sister Venus beat Czech Republic stars Andrea Hlavackova and Lucie Hradecka, bringing Serena four overall Olympic gold medal.

Williams needed to defeat her sister Venus to advance to Wimbledon's fourth round. She wanted to complete her trophy collection during this summer's 2015. Just a few days later she took the title in her final tennis match with Garbine Muguruza to win her second professional "Serena Slam" and established the Open record for the longest Grand Slam singles winner.

In this year's U.S. Open, Williams and Venus played each other in a close quarterfinal and Williams this time taking the victory at the end of the set in the final. She needed to win two more victories to win this calendar year Grand Slam, which has only been completed with three females in history tennis.

It wasn't to be however. The unseeded Roberta Vinci, ranked No. 43 worldwide, astonished everyone when she defeated Williams during the semis, 2-6 4-4, 6-4, 6-1.

Serena and Venus took home the doubles title at Wimbledon in 2016, just an hour after Serena was awarded tennis' singles championship. It is their 6th Wimbledon victory in all.

The Williams sisters suffered a shocking loss at the Rio Olympics in the women's doubles tournament in 2016. Czech teammates Lucie Safarova and Barbora Strycova defeated them during the first round. Their defeat was shocking because the Williams sisters were among the most favored players with an 15-0 Olympic record as well as three previous gold medals.

In this year's Australian Open, Williams made tennis history by beating her sister Venus by winning 6-4, 6-4, and 6-4, to take home the 23rd Grand Slam championship. Williams surpassed Steffi Graf's record of wins by winning her 23rd title which earned her the highest ranking in the world.

Williams spoke about her accomplishment and also cited the sister she had as her example. Venus is an amazing person and I'd like to use this opportunity to express my gratitude to her," the speaker said. "Without her, there's no way that I could be 23 years old today. Without her, I would never have achieved unity. She is the sole source of my motivation. I am the only reason for the Williams sisters are here and I am right here now."

Chapter 3: Journey To Success

1995-1998 Professional Debt

Williams Parents advised their daughter to put off competing in professional tournaments until she reached at least 16. Williams planned to make her debut as a professional in 1995 as a wild card entrant at the Bank of the West Classic in Oakland, California, but the WTA did not allow her to participate because of age eligibility rules.

Her parents asked her to withdraw her antitrust claim against the women's circuit in 1995, she did. In order to circumvent the age limit for eligibility she competed in her first competition, the Bell Challenge in Quebec in October 1995 to compete in her first professional event with a wild card entry.

With only two wins She lost to American Annie Miller, who was just 18 that time in the initial qualifying round.

Williams was absent from her 1996 campaign. She fell in the first round of three tournaments in the following year, but she won her first game at the top of the draw of the Ameritech Cup in Chicago on November. She beat No. 7. Mary Pierce and No. 4. Monica Sele when rated at the No. 304, securing her first victories in her career against top-ranked players. She also made history by being the only woman to beat two top-10 players in a single match in the Open Era.

In the end, he lost by No. five Lindsay Davenport in the semifinals. In 1997 she was rated as no. 99.

Williams began working in Medibank International Sydney in 1998. She was the 96th-ranked qualifier as well in quarterfinals, she defeated No. 3 Davenport before losing into Arantxa Sánchez Vicario, who was in the semifinals. In the Australian Open, Williams made her debut in the main draw of an official Grand Slam competition. In the first round, she defeated sixth seeded Irina Spirlea in the opening round, before losing against her younger twin sister Venus during the round two of the first match of professional competition between Williams and her sister. Williams sisters.

Through the course of the year she made it to six more quarterfinals, however she fell in all of them. These included her first encounter with Martina Hingis, who was ranked as No. 1 at the Lipton International Players Championships in Key Biscayne, and her second one , against Venus in the Italian Open in Rome.

The remainder of her year she failed to get beyond her round 16 at the same Grand Slam competition, falling to Arantxa Sanchez Vicario in Fourth round of the French Open and Spirlea in the third round of the US Open. She pulled out of Wimbledon due to a leg injury in the first game in the first set against Virginia Ruano Pascual. She as well as Max Mirnyi did win the mixed doubles championships at Wimbledon as well as in the US Open, capping the Williams family's stunning victory in the mixed doubles 1998 Grand Slam competitions.

Venus as well as Venus became the third duo of sisters to take home the WTA title at the U.S. National Indoor Championships in Oklahoma City, where she won her debut professional championship playing doubles. The year before, they also won two more doubles championships. Williams finished the year with a singles rank as No. 20.

BATTLE of the Sexes: KARSTEN BRAASCH VS. THE WILLIAMS SISTERS

In 1998, at the Australian Open, Serena and Venus at 16 old, participated in the tennis "Battle of the genders" with Karsten Braasch. Braasch is ranked at 203rd in the ATP at the time. The sisters took his offer, claiming they were able to beat any male who was not in his top 200.

Playing one match against each of the two, Braasch defeated them both. Venus defeated Serena 6-1 while Venus defeated Serena 6-2. Then Braasch said, "500 and beyond, you're not going to win." Later, the sisters altered the proportion to include people who weren't among the top 35 percent.

1999-2001 2001: STARTING TO BECOME A TOP-10 PLAYER

Williams lost to Sandrine Testud during the 3rd round at 1999's Australian Open. One month later, Williams upset Amelie Mauresmo in the Open Gaz de France final in Paris to win her first win as a professional singles player.

The two sisters became their first professional sisters who won tournaments during the same week, when Venus took home at the IGA Superthrift Classic in Memphis, Tennessee, on the same day. Williams beat Steffi Graf during the final event at the California Evert Cup in March of the year that she won her first Tier I victory. In the Miami Masters shortly after, Williams was beaten by her sister in the middle of her winning streak of 16 games in the first singles sister-versus-sister finale in WTA history. Williams was able to make her first appearance in the top-10 at No. 9.

Following that, she was afflicted with defeats in the third-round in the third round of the French Open, where she as well as Venus won the women's duo title, and the semifinals for the Italian Open and the German Open as well as at the Italian Open. Williams was injured and was unable to play Wimbledon.

Williams took home an Fed Cup singles match after returning to the circuit. She she went on to win the JPMorgan Chase Open in Los Angeles by beating Julie Halard Decugis in the final match. She then beat Grand Slam champions Monica Seles, Kim Clijsters, Conchita Martnez as well as Lindsay Davenport in quick succession in order to reach finals at the US Open final, where she beat the world's No. 1. Hingis to become the first American woman of African descent to take home the Grand Slam singles tournament after Althea Gibson in 1958.

The Williams sisters also won the doubles championship. Williams took home a doubles win during the Fed Cup final against Russia to conclude her 1999 season. In her only third full year on tour Williams was able to finish the year in fourth position.

Williams began her 2000 season by losing in the final to Elena Likhovtseva in the fourth round of the Australian Open. Even though she was the winner of in the Faber Grand Prix in Germany however, she was not able to hold her title at Paris as well as Indian Wells. Later, Williams' injury prevented her from participating at the French Open. Williams made her comeback during Wimbledon. Wimbledon Championships, where she lost to Venus in the semifinals , but the duo won the doubles title.

Williams won over Davenport in the final match of the championship to successfully keep the title she won to defend her title in Los Angeles. She played at her first Du Maurier Open final until she was forced to abandon the match against Hingis due to an injury. She was unable to retain the US Open crown after falling to Davenport in the semi-finals.

In September of the same year, Williams and Venus won the gold medal for doubles at the Sydney Olympics. Williams finished the year in sixth position after winning the Toyota Princess Cup in Japan.

in the semi-finals of both the Medibank International in Sydney and the Australian Open in Melbourne, Williams began the year falling to Martina Hingis. Williams as well as her sister won the doubles title at the finals and became the sixth duo to achieve the "Career Grand Slam" by winning the 4 Grand Slam women's doubles titles throughout their career. It was the Pacific Life Open in California was her next contest and she was crowned the title by beating Kim Clijsters.

The way fans have treated Williams along with her parents members during the final was a disaster for the tournament. Following the time that Venus pulled out of the final, the crowd was furious over the reported match fixing of games that involved family members.

For 14 years there was no way that Williams or her sister took part in the event; however, Williams joined as a wildcard in the year 2015. (and the highest seed). The following month, Williams was defeated by Jennifer Capriati in the quarterfinals of the Ericsson Open in Miami. Then, she was beaten at the hands of Capriati at the quarterfinals for both French Open and Wimbledon Championships. Williams has been eliminated from in the quarterfinals of a

Grand Slam competition in the quarterfinals four times in succession.

Williams was defeated by Monica Seriati in the final of the North American hard-court season in Los Angeles. Williams fell to the twin sister Venus at her US Open final of 2001. Then, during 2001, during the Open Era, the was the first Grand Slam event final in which two sisters were competing.

Williams was awarded the trophy with a walking over in the Tour Championships that ended the 2001 season following Davenport was forced to withdraw due to knee pain before the tournament even began. Williams was second, and then took home her first Rogers Cup for her second title of the season by defeating Cap001 at no. 6 for the second time in a row. year.

2002-2003: "SERENA SLAM"

The injury caused Williams to pull out of his participation at the Australian Open and the Medibank International Sydney semifinals in the beginning of 2002.

playing Amelie Mauresmo during the 2002 quarterfinals of the tournament in Sydney

Williams who was recovering of an injury beat the No. second Jennifer Capriati in the championship match for her first win this year on the court in Scottsdale, Arizona.

After defeating No. 3. Martina Hingis in the quarterfinals after defeating No. two Venus during the semis and No. one Jennifer Capriati in the final She won in the Miami Masters for the first time in history, becoming only three players from the Open Era to do so.

Venus lost to Serena by straight sets, for only the second time in her career.

Prior to 2003's French Open, Williams competed in three clay-court events. Williams entered her first event with

Charleston with the 3rd seed. Williams won against Patty Schnyder in the quarterfinals. She fell to Justine Henin in a three set tiebreak at the Eurocard German Open final, her first final on clay in May.

In the Italian Open, Williams went to take home her first clay court title after beating Capriati in the semifinals , and Henin in the final match. This resulted in her ranking climbed to a new record of No. 3.

Williams was the winner of her maiden title during the French Open at Roland Garros by beating Champion of the moment Capriati in the semis and the twin sister Venus winning the title in the final to claim the third Grand Slam event title. Williams was seeded third at the tournament (and her first time in two and a half years).

Williams has climbed to a record-setting position of No. 2. This was due to lifting the trophy in Court Philippe Chatrier and was ranked second to Venus.

Williams beat Venus to claim the Grand Slam singles title at the 2002 Wimbledon Championships for the first time in her career and without losing a set.

It was the longest tennis event Williams was able to win. Williams made her the third African American woman to occupy the world's number. #1 position in the wake of her win and relegated Williams' sister of the top spot. They also won the Williams sisters also took home the doubles championship during the event which gave them 5 Grand Slam doubles victories.

The time between Wimbledon between Wimbledon and between Wimbledon and the US Open, Williams competed in one tournament only and lost against American Chanda Rubin, in the semi-finals of the JPMorgan Chase Open in Los Angeles which ended a 21-match streak of winning. Williams was the highest-ranked participant of the US Open, advanced to the final and defeated her sister to take the title for the second time, her first US Open victory, for the third Grand Slam in a row.

Williams beat Kim Clijsters to win the Toyota Princess Cup in Tokyo and Anastasia Myskina to win the Sparkassen Cup in Leipzig, Germany in the fall of. Her winning streak of 18 matches was ended after she was defeated to her Home Depot Championships final at the Staples Center in Los Angeles against fifth seeded Kim Clijsters in straight sets.

Williams finished her year by securing a record of 56-5, a W/L total, 8 singles titles as well as the highest ranking. She took home three Grand Slam event championships in just one calendar year, which was the first in her career since Hingis in 1997. She became an African-American female the only one who has done this since Althea Gibson in 1958.
Williams became only the third tennis player to win the "Surface Slam," three Slam championships played on three

surfaces within that same year after Navratilova (1984) as well as Graf (1993 1995 1996) due to her three consecutive Grand Slam victories to conclude 2002.

Serena beat her sister in the final to claim the championship. She became the sixth woman during the Open Era to complete a career Grand Slam, joining Margaret Court, Billie Jean King, Chris Evert, Martina Navratilova as well as Steffi Graf. Serena took on Venus at the end of the match of the fourth time in a row at a Grand Slam tournament. She was also joined by Maureen Connolly Brinker, Court, Graf, and Navratilova as the sixth player to win every single Grand Slam singles championships concurrently.

The media called this feat as the "Serena Slam." In this tournament, the Williams sisters took home the sixth Grand Slam doubles championship as together.

Williams was the winner of the singles championships at The Open Gaz de France and the Sony Ericsson Open in the spring of 2003. After 21 wins, Williams' winning run was ended after she was defeated by Henin at finals of the Family Circle Cup final.

She also lost against Mauresmo in the Internazionali-BNL d'Italia semifinals, which took place in Rome. Williams was the top seed in the French Open despite these defeats and she lost to the eventual finalist Henin at the quarterfinals. It was her first loss in an official Grand Slam competition since 2001.

Williams challenged Henin's sporting skills in the game and the crowd was cheering for Williams her mistakes. After her loss in the French Open, Williams won the Wimbledon Championships, defeating Venus in the final, and Henin at the last quarterfinal. Williams was awarded six times all-time Grand Slam singles title and her second Wimbledon title consecutively with this victory.

Wimbledon was Williams the final game in 2003 following her withdrawal from three tournaments at the US and had quadriceps tendon surgery on her knee in the beginning of August. Williams was originally predicted to miss between six and eight weeks of competition.

2004-2007: INJURIES and THE RETURN

Williams began her return at her first NASDAQ-100 Open in Miami in March after a gap of eight months from the tour , during which her driving was under scrutiny. Williams made an impressive comeback with the title she won for the third time in consecutive years.

Williams was seeded second in the French Open despite being rated no. 7 overall, fell in the semifinals to Capriati during the semis, despite winning 4 games. In the years since Wimbledon 2002, Williams was undefeated in quarterfinals at the Grand Slam singles competition.

Williams was the highest player at Wimbledon the following week despite the fact her ranking had dropped to No. 10. To make it to in the semi-finals, She had to win six of her matches. In the final, 13th seeded Maria Sharapova beat her in straight sets. Her ranking dropped below that of the Top 10 players for the first time since 1999 , as a the result of her loss.

In the JPMorgan Chase Open in Los Angeles later in the summer, Williams advanced to her third final of the season and lost in the final to Lindsay Davenport, her first loss to one of an American after the 2001 US Open. Williams returned to in 2004 for the US Open after skipping her national event in 2003, and despite her ranking of at No. 11 in the world, she was seeded 3rd. The American was defeated in a controversial manner by Capriati 3 sets to 1 at the U.S. Open quarterfinals. Williams beat US Open winner Svetlana Kuznetsova in the China Open final for her second win of the year.

Williams Her outstanding campaign helped her to secure a place for Williams' impressive season earned her a spot in the Tour Championships, which were again hosted by Los Angeles. Williams made it to the final round even though she lost against Davenport as well as losing against Dementieva in round robin of the event. Williams won her semifinal, before losing against Sharapova in the final match, after she hurt her abdomen.

Williams was ranked at No. 7 by the end of 2004, however, she failed for the first time in her career since 2001 she was unable to win an Grand Slam singles title.

After Venus Williams' premature departure from the Australian Open, Williams vehemently denied that she as well as her sister were a declining player in tennis. The third round of the semifinal match, Williams beat Sharapova 8-6, after securing 3 match points. After winning 12 of the last 15 matches, Williams overcame top-seeded Davenport in the final, winning their third Australian Open and eighth Grand Slam singles title.

Williams declared she was striving to be in the top spot despite being dropped to the number. 2 after the victory.

The time between tennis' majors the Australian Open and Wimbledon, Williams only played in two tournaments. He lost against Venus at Miami as well as Francesca Schiavone at the Internazionali BNL d'Italia because of numerous withdrawals and retirements.

She wasn't able to play at the French Open due to a chronic ankle injury. Williams competed at Wimbledon again , this time as the fourth seed. However, Jill Craybas, ranked 85th was able to beat she in the 3rd round. Williams fell to sister Venus on the final day of the US Open. After their first encounter in 1998 at the Australian Open, this was Williams's first time competing in the Grand Slam competition.

Williams did not play in one match during the season, losing to No. No. 127 Sun Tiantian in the Beijing tournament. She was unable to compete in winning the season-ending title as the only time since the year 1998 and finished the year ranked 11th, the highest finish since 1998.

Williams made her debut at her debut at the Australian Open. Williams was competing to defend this title in 2006, got beaten by Daniela Hantuchova in the 3rd round. Williams claimed she was injured and reported it to the media after the event, blaming her absence from court for her inability to maintain fitness and knee injury.

Williams states in her memoir that she was depressed during that time. Through the 2006 season Williams took a six-month hiatus from tennis professional. Williams began going to a therapist each day following her decision to cut her off from the outside world for a time.

Williams was signed up to compete in Cincinnati the first time since Melbourne following a chance meeting with a young girl who loved Williams and believed she was still a possibility to succeed. Williams was down to No. 139, her lowest position since 1997. When she returned, Williams beat Myskina and Bethanie Mattek, before losing against Vera Zvonareva in the semifinals. When she was in Los Angeles, she too reached the semifinals, but lost to Jankovi with straight sets.

Williams needed a wildcard in order to participate for her first match at the US Open since, at the date of the cutoff Williams was in the 139th spot not far from the automatic 102 slot. At the time that the event began, her position was up to 79. The fourth time she played, she lost by the top seeded Mauresmo. She didn't play again in 2006 following she had lost in the US Open, finishing the year in the number. 95, which was her lowest ranking since 1997.

The 1987 Wimbledon singles champion for men along with expert Pat Cash called Williams' assertion that she was planning to rise back up the list "deluded" in the beginning of the year with greater confidence.

Williams was eliminated in the semifinals in the semifinals of Williams was eliminated in the semifinals of Hobart International, a tournament which served as an introduction to tennis' Australian Open where she was placed 81st and was considered to be "out in her form." Before the tournament Williams faced lots of criticism from her fans as well as the media and Williams herself for her weight, attention and determination to put in a great performance.

A Nike representative met her in the lounge of players prior to her first match and advised Williams that in the event that she did not perform to the standard she is used to the company might terminate her.

Williams stated that Nike's ultimatum demanded her to at minimum advance to the quarterfinals.

Williams didn't let attention from Nike stop her from overcoming Anne Kremer in straight sets and Mara Santangelo in just three games. Williams was suffering from a cold around the time, and had a blister formed in her heel. Williams was up against Nadia Petrova in the third round. She was just two points away from losing and she was able to prevail in three sets.

It was Williams her first win over the top-10 players after she beat Lindsay Davenport in the 2005 Australian Open final. Williams won against Jankovi, Peer and Vaidiova in the final match. Williams declared that the three were "excellent athletes. Strong competitors who certainly weren't expecting to play against an overweight, out of shape former champion such as myself." Williams was two points of losing to Peer before securing a comeback. Williams had a blister and cold was gone when she got to the final.

Although Williams enjoyed a great run, Tracy Austin predicted that the season was coming to an end and that Sharapova will easily beat Williams at the end of the tournament. Williams used it as an motivation, along with other criticisms and believed it to be rude and unjustified. Williams beat Maria Sharapova in the championship match with only three games lost, securing her first victory in a tournament since her 2004 Australian Open victory 24 months earlier.

Williams was crowned the third time she has won an Australian Open and ninth Grand Slam singles title overall she became the first athlete ever since Chris O'Neil to win the event without seeding. Williams is now 14th following her victory. Williams declared the title an honor towards her deceased half-sister and friend, Yetunde. The press praised her latest effort, describing it as "one among the most impressive tennis performances of all time" as well as "perhaps the most impressive performance ever seen in tennis for women."

Williams challenged her critics in an interview she conducted following the match, stating she had proven that they were incorrect. Williams won against Justine Henin to win victory at the Sony Ericsson Open in Miami for the fourth time. Williams was able to secure victory after losing the first set, and then winning 2 match point in the next.

In the Fed Cup match against Belgium She represented her country in the very first match since 2003. She took the first set, but was unable to play due to knee pain.

Williams fell to Henin during the semifinals at the French Open. Williams was unconscious after 5-5 in two sets of the Wimbledon game against Hantuchova at the end of the fourth set. The match was stopped for more than two hours due to the rain that fell following an emergency medical timeout, and she was forced to hold serve to create an end of tiebreak. Williams was victorious in three sets after players returned to the court.

Williams was subsequently unable to overcome Henin during the quarterfinals despite recovering from her injuries sustained in earlier in the round. Williams was beaten against Henin during the US Open quarterfinals, losing her third consecutive Grand Slam singles match. Williams participated for her first Kremlin Cup final but fell to Elena Dementieva.

Williams got a place at Williams's place in the WTA Championships, but she pulled out of her first tennis match with Anna Chakvetadze due to a knee problem. In the last time, Williams had the highest ranking of an American at the close of the year, coming in at the top of the list. 7.

2008-2010: REINVENTING THE TOP SPOT , AND INJURIES

At the beginning year 2008 Williams participated in the Mardy Fish led American team that took home the Hopman Cup. This was her fourth consecutive loss in the quarterfinals of an Grand Slam singles competition when she lost to Jelena Jankovi in the Australian Open.

Venus as well as Venus had to be eliminated in the doubles women's event during the quarterfinals. Williams has withdrawn from participation in the three following events because she needed urgent dental procedure.

Williams later won the fifth time in a row, winning her sixth Miami championship as well as three consecutive victories on her own at Bangalore she tied Steffi Graf as the record of most singles wins in this tournament.

This Family Circle Cup victory was Williams the first victory on clay since 2002's French

Open. Dinara Safina ended her winning streak of 17 matches during the Berlin quarterfinals. Because of a back problem, Williams withdrew from the quarterfinal with Alize Cornet, who was playing in Rome. Williams had the distinction of being the one former French Open champion in the draw, but she lost to Katarina Srebotnik in the third round.

The elder sister of Venus beat Williams with ease to win the first Slam final since 2003's Wimbledon in which she reached Finals in the past the past four years. This was the first time since 2003 that Serena as well as Venus were the winners of the ladies doubles title as in a group. Williams was a student at Stanford in the past, walked out of the semifinals against qualifying player Aleksandra Wozniak, after she fell behind 6-2, 3-1, due to an injury to her knee. Williams had to withdraw from Los Angeles due to the injuries.

Williams was defeated by Dementieva to reach the quarterfinals in Williams lost to Dementieva in the quarterfinals of Beijing Olympics. In the final of doubles, Serena and Venus defeated Anabel Medina Garrigues as well as Virginia Ruano Pascual to claim the gold medal. Williams took home her first US Open after defeating Jelena Jankovi, Safina, and her sister Venus in the final. Williams' 3rd US Open triumph and ninth Grand Slam singles crown came from the tournament.

The first time in a while since the 2003 she was able to return to the top spot with the win. She beat Safina and fell to Venus in the round-robin match in the championships of the year's end and then pulled out of the match against Dementieva due to stomach muscle issue.

With four singles titles as well as the No. 2 position at the conclusion of the year She had her greatest year since 2003.

The Medibank International that kicked off with, Williams lost to Elena Dementieva in the semifinals. Williams defeated Dinara Safina to win the Australian Open singles final in 60 minutes to take home her 10th Grand Slam title. By winning she was able to return to the top spot and overtake golfer Annika Sorenstam for her place as women's tennis all-time top player in the amount of prize money earned in a career. They took the title in women's doubles along with Venus three times.

Williams pulled out of her participation in the Open GdF Suez due to an injury to her knee prior to her semi-final game against Dementieva.

Then, Serena competed in Dubai but came up short against Venus in the semifinals.

Williams who was affected by quad and ankle issues, was defeated by Victoria Azarenka in the Sony Ericsson Open final. Williams then went on to have the longest losing streak of her career, with four consecutive losses. In her first games held in Barcelona, Rome, and Madrid she was beaten. She was defeated by eventual winner Svetlana Kuznetsova, in semis despite not having played on clay in 2009.

Her winning streak over her 18 Grand Slam matches came to an end because of. In Wimbledon Serena recovered and beat fourth seeded Dementieva by securing the match point. Serena took home the Wimbledon title and also it was her eleventh Grand Slam singles title by beating Venus, her twin sibling Venus at the end of her match.

For the second time in a row, Serena and Venus won the women's doubles tournament at Wimbledon and have an overall record of 9 Grand Slam victories in the category.

Williams played in Cincinnati as a warm-up to her participation in the US Open but lost there in the third round. Williams then fell at her Rogers Cup semifinals.

In the US Open, Williams was accused of shouting at a line judge when fighting a match point that cost her the point and, ultimately, the match. The American lost to eventual champion Kim Clijsters in the quarterfinals. Then she won her doubles final, playing alongside Venus to win their 11th consecutive Grand Slam doubles championship and third of the year.

Williams beat Venus, Dementieva, and Kuznetsova as she won each of her round-robin matches in the year-end WTA Tour Championships. She also escaped losing the set point in a match to Venus. In the event that Wozniacki pulled out of the semifinal match, she then moved on to the final match. Williams won the tournament's second singles title after beating Venus in the final match.

With 16 tournaments played, which is more than ever before, Williams ended the season with a ranking of no. 1. For the second consecutive time throughout her professional career. Williams was awarded $6,545,586 of cash prizes, surpassing the previous record of Justine Henin of the largest sum an female tennis player has ever received during the course of a calendar year. Even though they only played six matches as a team during the year they Williams sisters ended their year ranked as No. 2 in doubles.

Williams had won the number of Grand Slam championships after winning five Grand Slam event wins, and the Associated Press honored her Female Athlete of the Year in 2009. Williams also took home the doubles and singles championships at the ITF World Championships.

In Sydney in the year 2010, Williams competed in her first match of the year, but lost against Elena Dementieva in the championship match. Williams was the reigning doubles and singles champions of The Australian Open. She made it to the final , and then won her 10th Grand Slam singles championship by beating Justine Henin, who had just come out of retirement.

Williams along with her twin sister Venus took home the doubles title by beating Cara Black and Liezel Huber in the final match.

Williams pulled out of her next events because of injuries to her leg. She then made her return in The Rome Masters, where she was beaten by Jelena Jankovi, in the semi-finals. Williams lost to Nadia Petrova in the third round in Madrid however she joined with Venus to take home the doubles title.

Williams fell to Samantha Stosur in the quarterfinals of the French Open. She as well as Venus were among the top seeded players for the doubles event and won first place after defeating Kvta Peschke as well as Katarina Srebotnik during the final match. They went on to take home their fourth consecutive Grand Slam doubles championship and climb into the upper echelons of doubles ranking.

Williams played at Wimbledon in which she beat Russian Vera Zvonareva in the final match, never being forced to play a break point , and she succeeded in she broke her serve three times. In all the matches Williams did not drop one set.

After this match Martina Navratilova claimed that Serena Williams is among the most outstanding five tennis women of all time "Your entire performance is far more significant than the number of Slams or competitions you've won.

She has every advantage." For doubles play, Serena along with her twin sister Venus were champions of the year after winning in the last two years. The pair were defeated Elena Vesnina and Veronareva in the quarterfinals. Williams was injured on July 7 , in Munich after walking onto a glass that had shattered in the restaurant, causing Williams to be out for the rest of the season.

After six tournaments, Williams finished the year at no. 4 in singles, and No. 11 in doubles.

She admitted to the presence of a hematoma, as well as an embolism in the pulmonary vein on March 2nd 2011.

2011-2013: RECOVERING SUPREMACY and A Career Slam

In March of 2011, Williams at last returned to the court for practice. In Eastbourne Williams returned back to playing on the WTA tour after more than one year. In a match that lasted over 3 hours Williams lost to Vera Zvonareva in the second round. Wimbledon is her following tournament and she was there to defend her title at Wimbledon.

She made it into the round of 16 and was defeated by Marion Bartoli defeated her. Following her defeat she was ranked number 169. Williams won both in

Stanford as well as Toronto to secure her first win since returning to tennis. Williams was a major upset Lucie Hradecka during The Western & Southern Open before taking a break the following day because of an injury to her right foot. Williams later played in the US Open, reaching the final where she was defeated by Samantha Stosur in a match that saw her aggressively abuse her chair umpire.

Williams' final game of the year came in her US Open final, and she was ranked no. 12 with two championships , and overall a record of 22-3. Through the entire season, she participated in six events.

In the Brisbane International, where she began her 2012 season, Williams suffered a left ankle injury while playing in an opponent in the game in the match against Bojana Jovanovski. Williams was forced to quit the tournament due to this. Williams then played in an event called the Australian Open where Ekaterina Makarova defeated her during the 4th round. Williams returned to play at Miami after a break of a month but was beaten in the quarterfinals by Caroline Wozniacki in the quarterfinals.

After beating Lucie Afakova, and Victoria Azarenka, Williams won two championships, at Charleston as well as Madrid. But, she pulled out of her final game in Rome against Li Na in Rome due to an injury to her lower back. In the French Open, Williams lost to Virginie Razzano in the opening round, for only the second time she has ever lost in her entire career. Williams took home five championships along the course of building 33-1 in the second quarter of her season. Williams broke the record for serving of 24 aces for women in a single match, and also had the highest number of Aces in all competitions. She then won five times at Wimbledon singles title as well as her 14th Grand Slam title. In her return in America, United States, Williams overcame CoCo Vandeweghe in the final game at Stanford to win her title.

Following that, Williams went back to Wimbledon to get ready to make her Olympic debut. There, she took home gold after a rout of Maria Sharapova in a commanding performance. Williams was awarded the gold medal for not losing any more than 3 games in one set. Williams was unbeaten for the entire time, but it was ended in the final match against Angelique Kerber, in Cincinnati.

Williams beat Azarenka during her New York City final to win her 4th US Open singles championship and her 15th Grand Slam title overall. Williams took part in her first WTA Championships to round up the regular season, winning the tournament and winning the tournament for the third time. Williams got an eighth consecutive vote to be the WTA player of the Year.

Williams was also named World Champion in 2012. International Tennis Federation World Champion due to her exceptional performances in the 2012. Williams and

Venus have also returned to doubles competitions and in their first game since Wimbledon in 2010, they won their 13th grand Slam doubles title as well as their fifth Wimbledon doubles title. Williams and Venus became tennis' first players to win four gold medals, after successfully winning their Olympic doubles title.

Williams took the title in Brisbane her first competition of 2013 without dropping a single set. American tennis player Sloane Stephens defeated Williams in the Australian Open quarterfinals. Williams returned to the number. one at the age of six following beating Petra Kvitova in Doha, becoming an oldest female to hold the title during the Open Era. Williams lost in the final to Victoria Azarenka in the championship match.

Williams lost her first loss in a set in eight years when she lost against Maria Sharapova in the Miami final. Williams won her 70th come from behind victory despite the loss. Williams made her fourth person during the Open Era to have won an event more than six times. She won the event beating the record set by Steffi Graf with six wins in Miami.

Williams took home Williams the Charleston championship for the third time in a row after winning the title. The following year in Madrid, Williams defeated Sharapova to claim her 50th singles crown overall. Williams then played in Rome and won the title without losing one set. At the end of her match, Williams beat Victoria Azarenka in her second final to win the championship. Williams did not lose more than 10 games in her time in Roland Garros to go to the quarterfinals. Williams faced Svetlana Kuznetsova in the quarterfinals and lost her first set of the tournament.

Chris Evert, a seven-time French Open winner, called Williams her quarterfinal win over Sara Errani, in which she lost only one game--"the most impressive woman's performance on clay she's ever witnessed." To win the third Roland Garros championship and her 15th grand Slam overall, Williams overcame Sharapova.

She joins Navratilova, Evert, and Graf as the only female during the Open Era to have won every Grand Slam event title at least once. She was comfortably through to the Wimbledon fourth round only to lose to the eventual Champion Sabine Lisicki in three sets. After Wimbledon, Williams won the Swedish Open by beating Johanna Larsson in the final. It is the very first time Williams had ever taken home an international title. level. Williams could stay unbeaten on clay throughout the entire season, winning the event.

Williams won over Sorana Cirstea during The Rogers Cup final to win her third title in Toronto. Williams made her debut appearance at the Western & Southern Open final but was defeated by Azarenka. Williams was the highest seeded and the defending champion at the US Open.

Williams advanced to the final in which she played Azarenka in a reprise from the final in 2012 she won three sets to take home her seventeenth Grand Slam singles championship.

Williams raised her career award amount to $50 million and was the longest-running US Open champion in the Open Era. Williams beat Jelena Jankovi in the China Open in Beijing following the US Open, giving her 10 wins in 2013. Williams won the title contest with Li Na to go unbeaten in the WTA Championships and became the first champion since Justine Henin in 2007 to be able to defend her title. Williams became the 8th player to win 11 titles or more in one year, and only the second to do so since Martina Hingis in 1997 when she won her 11th championship in 2013.[]

Williams also became the fourth person to take home the WTA Championships four times or more and was the oldest player to accomplish this feat. With her win,

Williams became the first female player to earn more than $10 million in one season. Her total was $12,385,572 just Novak Djokovic and Rafael Nadal have made more money in the same year.

Williams was the first player in history to be the highest-ranked player in WTA history, after completing the calendar year with the title of No. one player for the third time. Williams was also crowned as 2013 ITF World Champion, earning the title for the fourth time. In the 2013 ESPY Awards, Williams took home two prizes. Williams won the title of the top female tennis player and female athlete. Williams was awarded the title of Best Female Tennis Player for a record six times and is only the fourth woman to be awarded Best Female Athlete on two different occasions. Williams finished the year by receiving the 2013 Female Athlete of the Year award from the Associated Press in late December.

It marks her the third AP distinction following the awards she received in 2002 and 2009. Since the first AP Athlete of the Year award was announced in 1931 just two ladies, Chris Evert and Babe Didrikson were awarded this honor more often.

SECOND "SERENA SLAMM" In 2014-2015

Williams defeated No. 2. Victoria Azarenka in the Brisbane International championship match to keep her crown. She was defeated by the former No. one Ana Ivanovic during the 4th round at the Australian Open. Alize Cornet beat Williams with a straight set in the semi-finals in the Dubai tournament. Williams went on to Miami and beat No. 2. Li Na in straight sets to win her record-breaking ninth crown.

Williams lost to Jana epelova in the Family Circle Cup second round. Williams was a participant at Madrid Open. Madrid Open until she withdrew due to a left hip injury. In Rome, Williams won her third title for the season. Garbie Muguruza then handed her the biggest loss during his Grand Slam tournament career. At the end of round three at Wimbledon, Alize Cornet upset Williams for the second time this year, leading Williams losing for the very first time in Wimbledon since 2005.

In the midst of falling behind by 0-3 points during the 2nd round of doubles contest together with their twin sister Venus, Serena was forced to end her match. After being removed from what is described as one of the most bizarre tennis events ever witnessed and a confused Serena had four consecutive double errors and was experiencing issues with her ball throw and movement.

Williams won back her title by winning in the next 19 of her 20 matches (losing only to her sister Venus in the semi-finals in The Rogers Cup). It also included wins in the Bank of the West Classic as well as her first victory of the Western & Southern Open, and her third straight , and the sixth time overall US Open singles victory, which she won without losing a set. In her victory, Williams matched Chris Evert's record for the most singles women's titles won at the US Open during the Open Era.

Williams also set his Open Era record for most Grand Slam singles championships (18) together with Evert as well as Navratilova. Williams was awarded $4 million following her win at both the US Open and US Open Series making it the biggest prize in the history of tennis. Williams was on break in the first game against Alize Cornet in the Wuhan Open when a viral illness forced her to stop playing. So, Cornet was the only woman ever since Justine Henin's 2007 win to beat Williams three times during the calendar year.

Before playing Samantha Stosur in the quarterfinals of the China Open, Williams announced her retirement. Despite suffering an injury setback against Simona Halep, in round two of 2014's WTA Finals in Singapore that equaled her career-high, Williams made it to the final for the second year in the same row. Williams took revenge for her loss to Halep during the semifinals, winning the fifth WTA Finals crown and eighth finals title of the season. In her fourth career win, Williams was ranked top at the close this year.

Nhe retained her No. number one ranking throughout the year, something that Steffi Graf was last seen doing in 1996. In addition, she was voted to be WTA Player of the Year and ITF World Champion for a third time in a row (sixth in the overall rankings).

Williams as well as John Isner represented the United States in John Isner and Williams represented the United States at Hopman Cup to kick off the 2015 season. The Polish team beat the American pair at the end of the match. Williams took home her sixth Australian Open singles championship for the sixth time and won the 19th Grand Slam singles title of her career after defeating Maria Sharapova for the 16th consecutive time. She won it with her third point of the match of second match. Williams is now the record holder for the second-highest number of Grand Slam singles championships won during the Open Era, trailing only Navratilova and Evert.

At the age of 30 she has taken home the title of six Grand Slam singles championships, three more than her closest rival (Margaret Court, Martina Navarratilova with three wins each). Serena is the only athlete in history to record at the very least 1 Grand Slam victory after turning 30. In the following weekend, Serena and her sister Venus traveled for Buenos Aires to compete against Argentina in an Fed Cup World Group II match.

She played in and won her single tennis match with Mara Irigoyen to assist Team USA in beating Argentina 4-1. Williams has ended her 14-year ban at Indian Wells

Masters after 14 years of boycott. Indian Wells Masters by announcing that she will be taking the court in the tournament. Williams returned to a huge cheer from the crowd and won her first match with straight sets.

She reached the semifinals, and was set to face No. 3 Simona Halep to be a participant in the finals However, she was forced to withdraw due to knee injuries. Only the eighth female player of tennis's Open Era to have 700 matches throughout the course of her playing career. Williams made it happen after beating Sabine Lisicki in the Miami Open quarterfinals.

She's now only three active players --the others being Rafael Nadal and Roger Federer--to have more than 700 singles wins. She beat Halep at the quarterfinals and advanced to her 11th final of the tournament in which she beat Carla Suarez Navarro to win an eighth title that set a record and extend her winning streak to 21 games.

Williams went on a trip to Brindisi, Italy, to play against Italy's team for an opportunity to be part of the Fed Cup's World Group in order to be prepared for clay court play (and to ensure her participation in at the Olympics in 2016 Summer Olympics). Williams as well as Alison Riske fell to Sara Errani and Flavia Pennetta in the crucial doubles game, and as an outcome that Williams was dropped from the United States team was demoted to World Group II.

Williams was the first player to suffer a Fed Cup defeat. Williams defeated Camila Giorgi as well as Errani to keep her record of singles undefeated. Williams's 114th consecutive week as No. 1 on April 20th was the third longest streak in WTA record, only a few weeks behind Steffi Graf's 186 weeks as well as Martina Navastrilova's 155.6. Williams fell to No. four Petra Kutova, in the semifinals in the Mutua Madrid Open, handing her her first loss of the season.

This loss ended to Williams his 27-match winning streak and a 50-match winning streak in Premier-Mandatory tournamentsand a 19-match winning streak during the particular event. Before withdrawing from the Internazionali BNL d'Italia in 2015 due to an elbow injury Williams participated in one match.

Williams was the very first female during tennis's Open Era to win 50 matches in all four Grand Slams following beating Victoria Azarenka in the third round of the French Open. Following that, Williams overcame Sloane Stephens to make it to the 40th Grand Slam quarterfinal in singles. Williams beat her opponent in the next round, however, to make it to the semifinals with Timea Bacsinszky, in the semis Williams needed to recover from defeat to win four times in the same matches. Williams would later claim her third French Open of her career and her 20th Grand Slam singles title by beating Czech Republic's Lucie Afaova, in three sets.

In winning, Williams joined Margaret Court and Steffi Graf as the sole players who have won the Grand Slam at least three times. Because she did it herself in the Serena Slam, she is the only person to win three consecutive Grand Slams. She is also the first player ever since Jennifer Capriati in 2001 to take home the double of the French Open and Australian Open.

Lmk Williams was the winner of her first title at the 2015 Wimbledon Championships which is winning her 6th Wimbledon and her 21st Grand Slam singles championship, to complete her second "Serena Slam" (winning all four Grand Slams consecutively). It was especially difficult to achieve her victory at Wimbledon. After rallying to win and becoming the first player to make it to WTA Finals WTA Finals, she was two points away from losing twice and was a step behind Heather Watson by a double break in the third round (the first time an athlete was able to qualify since the tournament changed to a round-robin format at the end of 2003). Venus Williams, Victoria Azarenka along with Maria Sharapova were the next three former No. one players Williams lost to in succession to make it to the championship game.

She discovered Garbie Muguruza who was a 21-year-old athlete who had earlier handed Williams the most devastating Grand Slam tournament loss of her career during the 2014 French Open, there waiting for her. Muguruza fell to Williams in a tough two-set contest.

Williams was the oldest woman to win an individual grand slam title during the Open Era as well as the oldest woman to take home an individual grand slam title in the history of tennis due to the victory. Williams was also able to break Steffi Graf's Open Era record of seven wins in a row between 1995 and 1999. She also equaled Pete Sampras's Open Era record of eight wins from 1995 to 2000 for the most wins in a row at Grand Slam singles finals.

The 21 Grand Slam singles championships were more than all other women's circuit players. In the very first instance during WTA record, the most successful player had more than two times as many points than the second-placed player during the week ending on July 13. Williams was awarded the Best Female Tennis Player ESPY for the seventh time following her win at Wimbledon.

Before resigning from for the Swedish Open in Bstad due to an injury to her elbow, Williams played one match. Williams was the reigning champion in the Bank of the West Classic however she pulled out in order to let her elbow heal. In three tightly fought sets during the Canadian Open semifinals, 18-year-old Swiss Belinda Bencic, the number. 20, stopped Williams' 19-match winning run. The first loss for the season was on hard courts and it was her first loss in a while since her WTA Finals of 2014. Williams took home her the 69th WTA title in the next week when she beat No. 3. Simona

Halep, in straight-sets during the Western & Southern Open, breaking an unbroken tied with Evonne Goolagong for fifth place in the number of WTA victories she won by herself.

Williams attempts to complete the "Grand Slam"--winning the entire of the four Grand Slam tournaments in a single calendar year -- was unsuccessful after she was defeated in the quarterfinals of Roberta Vinci in the US Open quarterfinals. Many have called the loss one of the greatest tennis shocks of all time.

But, Williams' performance at the event made sure that she'd finish her year as the number. 1 player. Williams declared the end of her campaign on the 1st of October explaining that she'd suffered from illness for the majority of the year and required to pay attention to her health. Before the decision, Williams' coach Patrick Mouratoglou suggested that she wouldn't return to tennis in 2015 as she was dismotivated and unhappy following her Open defeat.

On the 5th of October, Williams passed Chris Evert to claim the record for the third most weeks as the top-ranked athlete. Williams placed as the first player for her sixth career. She maintained the top spot throughout throughout the season for the second consecutive year. In addition, for the 8th time, the tennis player was awarded the WTA player of the Award of the Year. Williams was named WTA's Sportsperson of the Year on the 14th of December.

The first female to receive this award, which was first awarded in 1983. She was also only the third female to receive the award by herself.

Williams was also awarded the sixth title in her professional career, which she won as ITF World Champion. Then it was announced that she had been awarded the The Associated Press's female Athlete of the Award for a unprecedented fourth consecutive time.

OPEN ERA GRAND SSLAM Record for 2016

After she quit the singles game in the singles match against Australia Gold due to left knee pain, Williams withdrew from the Hopman Cup. It was the Australian Open, where she was the reigning champion as well as the highest seeded is her next tournament.

She beat world number. 4 Agnieszka Radwanska, as well as world the world's no. five Maria Sharapova en route to the final in which she was up against the first-time Grand Slam finalist Angelique Kerber. Since she'd never been defeated in a semifinal or final of the Australian Open, she was considered the most likely to win the tournament. With just one set loss over six games and no set losses over 4 years of playing, she beat them head-to-head.

Kerber took home her first Grand Slam championship, while Williams lost in the final by three sets. Williams lost her first ever three-set defeat in the Grand Slam final and her first defeat at the Australian Open. She previously held records of 8-0 and 6-0.

Williams beat Martina Navratilova's record for 156 consecutive months at No. 1 to set the record for the second-longest run in WTA history, second only to Steffi Graf's record of 186 during that week on February 15. She played as the top seed at Indian Wells.

After defeating Simona Halep during the quarterfinals, and Agnieszka Radwanska, in her semifinals. She progressed into her very first final the venue since winning in 2001 before abstaining from the event. As she made it towards the semifinals, she fell only one set. Williams fell to the no. 13-seed Victoria Azarenka, who she had defeated in straight sets in the five previous times they had met.

Williams The two consecutive defeats in the finals were a the first time since. Williams then played for The Miami Open while holding the title. The fourth time she played she lost to Svetlana Kuznetsova. Her winning streak of 20 matches in Miami ended in this match, and it was her first loss since the year 2012. It also marked her fastest exit from this event since she lost in the same round back in 2000.

Williams was forced to leave Madrid in the clay court swing , but moved to Rome. She defeated Christina McHale and Anna-Lena Friedsam to make it to the quarterfinals in which she beat Svetlana Kuznetsova in order to get revenge for her Miami defeat. Then she was able to beat Madison Keys and Irina-Camelia Begu to take home her first WTA champion of the year , and also winning the 70th WTA trophy overall. She was fourth overall and third place in Rome over the past four years.

Williams only lost one set during her final match at the French Open his route to the title. Although she was five points of winning Williams, she fought off Yulia Putintseva to reach the quarterfinals.

After overcoming a surprise finalist Kiki Bertens, she made it into her 4th French Open final, where she faced Garbie Muguruza in an rematch of her Wimbledon final from last year in which Williams was victorious.

Contrary from in the Wimbledon final Williams was defeated by Muguruza by straight sets during this game. In this loss, Williams became the first player in her career to lose consecutive Grand Slam finals. After this loss, Williams not only failed to equal Steffi Graf's Open Era record of 22 Grand Slam singles victories, but she also ended with a runner-up finish in the Career Grand Slam runner-up set.

Williams just dropped one set in Wimbledon before advancing to her final match against Angelique Kerber, which was a rematch the Australian Open final from earlier in the year. Williams won against Kerber the second time with straight sets, and ultimately tie Steffi Graf's mark of 23 Grand Slam victories during the Open Era.

It was Williams's seventh WTA championship in all in addition to her very first Grand Slam victory of the year. Williams only missed one break point during the entire game against Kerber due to her superb serving skills, which she was able to avoid by hitting an ace. Williams as well as her sister Venus took home the sixth time Wimbledon doubles title, and their 14th overall duo Grand Slam trophy later that day, securing their unbeaten record in Grand Slam doubles finals.

Williams pulled out of Williams' participation in Rogers Cup on July 24 in 2016, citing an injury to her shoulder. Then, she competed at her first Rio de Janeiro Olympics, in which she won the title of the reigning world champion doubles and singles and was the most popular choice to repeat her gold medal. Along with her sister Venus she were 15-0 in their lifetime dating through the 2000 Olympics before losing in the finals to the Czech team comprised of Lucie Afaova and Barbora Strcova during the first stage of doubles tournament.

In the singles event in the singles competition, following victories against Daria Gavrilova as well as Alize Cornet during the opening round, Serena Williams faced Ukrainian Elina Svitolina in the third round of the same matchup as that of the 4th round in the French Open. Williams lost to Svitolina, the Ukrainian losing the Ukrainian's Olympic campaign.

A few days after that Olympics, Williams accepted a late wildcard to play at the Western & Southern Open, which she won as the champion in her final year, however she pulled out due to concerns over the same shoulder injury and injury that she suffered previously in summer.

Williams' 186th consecutive week at No. 1 on the 5th of September 2016, was tied with Steffi Graf's record of the most longest stretch of consecutive weeks WTA history.

Karolna Plkova beat Williams during Williams's defeat in the US Open semifinals. Angelique Kerber who was the winner of in the US Open, overtook Venus Williams as the world's No. 1 player, breaking her reign. Williams pulled out of WTA Finals. WTA Finals as well due to an injury to her shoulder.

AUSTRALIAN OPEN TRIUMPH AND PREGNANCY in 2017

Williams played in her first WTA Auckland Open for the first time in her career , to begin her 2017 campaign. She won her first tournament after she won the US Open by defeating Pauline Parmentier.

She was unable to overcome Madison Brengle in the next round. She was defeated by Belinda Bencic, Lucie afaova, Johanna Konta, and other Australian Open competitors to advance to her eighth Australian Open final. She beat their twin sister Venus in the final on 28 January 2017 to be the winner of the Australian Open for a record-breaking seventh time during the Open Era. She has surpassed Steffi Graf's Open Era record of 22 Grand Slam singles victories and she now holds 23.

Two players of 35 years old or older were part of an Grand Slam final for the first time in the Open Era. Williams was guaranteed a place in the top spot thanks to her win. Williams then pulled out due to knee pain at an injury sustained at the Indian Wells and Miami Opens.

Williams declared on April 19 on the 19th of April, 2017 that she was pregnant for 20 weeks and was out for the remainder season. Williams was between 8 and 9 weeks pregnant when she took home in the Australian Open, based on the date she announced her pregnancy.

She said in interviews that she had an "outrageous strategy" to participate at her first tournament in the year 2018 at the Australian Open when she returned to tennis after her pregnancy.

Alexis Olympia Ohanian, Jr., Williams' daughter was born on the 1st of September 2017. However, she is not technically a junior as Kerry was her dad's middle initial. She is known as Olympia.
In labor she suffered an embolism in her lungs, which required an emergency cesarean section. After giving birth after which she suffered a second an embolism in her lungs, making her in bed for 6 weeks and put her off returning to her training.

Williams was defeated by the current French Open winner Jeena Ostapenko in her first game after giving birth to her daughter on Dec. 30, 2017 during an exhibition match at the World Tennis Championship in Abu Dhabi.

2018 Return to tennis and WIMBLEDON RUNNER-UP. THE US OPEN

Williams has pulled out of the Australian Open on January 5 the 5th of January, 2018. She cited insufficient training due to her pregnancy.

After overcoming her pregnancy-related health issues She as well as her sister returned to the tennis courts in February. The 11th of February, the pair were defeat against Lesley Kerkhove and Demi Schuurs (Netherlands) in the first round of the Fed Cup.

Williams declared that she was at ease to play tennis again However, she was knocked out early in the tournaments of Indian Wells and Miami, losing against Venus Williams in the third round of Indian Wells and Naomi Osaka in the first round in Miami.

Williams played doubles and singles along with their twin sister Venus during the 2017 French Open to make her return back to Grand Slam tennis. Williams defeated Kristna Plkova in the opening round with two sets that were close and then beat 17th-seed Ashleigh Barty in round two.

Then, she defeated top seed Julia Gorges to earn a match against the 28th seed Maria Sharapova, whom she had defeated previously 18 times from 2004. Williams pulled out because of a pectoral muscle strain that she sustained in an doubles match in the third round , the third round, where she along with Venus fell to Andreja Klepa, and Mara Jose Martnez Sanchez.

Williams participated in Williams played in the Wimbledon Championships in July and was seeded at a tense #25. He had a world rating of 181 there was a consensus that the decision was biased and disproportionately favors Williams.

Others argued their argument that All England Club, which doesn't base its seeds on world rankings, unlike other grand slam competitions -- had intelligently took into account Williams's impressive previous performance at the tournament. Williams stated: "I had a wonderful surprise. I went to the event with the thought that I could not receive the seed." Dominika Cibulkova did not get her place to be seeded because due to her seeds.

The first time ever in the history of grand slams that none of the top 10 female players are in the quarterfinals in the end of week two in competition. Williams beat Arantxa Rus from Holland at the beginning of round 1, Viktoriya Tomova from Bulgaria at the second round, Kristina Mladenovic of France in round three and Evgeniya Rodina from Russia during round four, to move on into the semifinals. At this point, she'd never lost one set at any point in her match.

After losing only one match, Williams defeated Italian Camila Giorgi in the quarterfinals in order to reach the semifinals of Wimbledon as the tennis player with the lowest ranking ever. In the semifinals she took on Germany's 13th-ranked Julia Gorges, who she easily beat in two sets, advancing to her 10th Wimbledon final and the first since having a child.

In a reprise of the Wimbledon title in 2016 she was defeated against German Angelique Kerber, who won the championship, in straight sets.

Williams participated in her first tournament of the year, Silicon Valley Classic after her race to the Wimbledon finals. It was her first appearance in an US Open Series event since the year 2015. Only winning one game in the first round against Johanna Konta in the opening round, she fell to the most lopsided loss in her professional career.

Williams then acknowledged in an interview with Time interview that 10 minutes prior to the time the match began, she went to Instagram and saw that the man who killed and shot the half sister of her, Yetunde in the year 2003, was released by parole at the time of her death. The interviewer admitted, "I couldn't get that out of my mind."

It was the Cincinnati Masters was Williams' next tournament. She won the opening round and beat the Australian Daria Gavrilova with straight sets. However, in her second match, she got beaten in three sets by Petra Kvitova in a three-set match that lasted for more than two hours. While she was ranked as 26th on the WTA rankings at the time the seeds were allocated and the seeding for her was 17th to play in this year's US Open in Flushing Meadows, New York.

She knocked out the 16th seed Kaia Kanepi, 16th seed in the final round. the eighth seeds Karolna Plkova to reach the semifinals. Magda Linette from the opening round Carina Witthoft, in round two and the sister of Venus at the end of round three as well as Venus at the end of fourth. The match was a replay of Plkova's final US Open match from 2016 that Plkova was the winner.

After her return from pregnancy This was Williams's first win over any of the world's top players (at the moment that the game took place). Williams beat Latvia's Anastasija Sevastova, a 19th seed in the semifinals match in order to reach the women's singles final in which she lost against Japan's Naomi Osaka in straight sets. Williams was given a warning for inappropriate coaching as well as a deduction of one point for breaking her racket as well as a game penalty for verbally assaulting her chair umpire.

2019 Return to TOP 10: SETBACKS, RUNNERS UP, SETBACKS WIMBLEDON FINISHES and THE US OPEN

Williams began her season in 2019 with The Australian Open, where she has not played since she took the title in the 2017 tournament. She made it to the quarterfinals to the quarterfinals against Tatjana Maria Eugenie Bouchard as well as Dayana Yastremska in the initial 3 rounds, seeded 16th before overcoming Simona Halep, the highest seed and the current world number one in the fourth round. She played seventh-seeded Karolna Plkova in the quarterfinals.

Plkova took the first set and held the lead in the second set, however Williams quickly took over the match after taking the set in its second before taking a lead into the third. Plkova did win six consecutive matches and held off four match points throughout the set to win the match after Williams was injured in her ankle as she serving to win the win.

Williams lost in the first round at the Australian Open for the first time since she lost to the 4th round of 2014, ending a streak of 14 straight wins at the Grand Slam quarterfinals (having last lost an Grand Slam quarterfinal at the 2013 Australian Open). Despite the loss she climbed up to number 11.

In her quest for the third Indian Wells title, Williams was able to defeat Victoria Azarenka in the second round of the Indian Wells Masters. Williams had to pull out of the game against Spaniard Garbie Muguruza during the final round because of a viral infection.

She was forced to leave at this time for the second time in succession. Then she experienced the recurrences of a knee injury that was chronic, requiring her to pull out of Miami as well as Rome following just one game. After she played in the French Open, where she was eliminated at the end of round three she was unable to properly train.

Williams was able to reach an important Final at Wimbledon for the 13th year in a row. Williams was also the open's longest-running grand finalist in the slam. Simona Halep beat her in the final match with just less than an hour and two sets.

In the Canadian Open, Williams defeated Marie Bouzkova of the Czech Republic in the semifinals of the tournament in three sets following her defeat of Naomi Osaka in straight sets in the quarterfinals. Williams was defeated in the opening game of the match against Canadian teenager Bianca Andreescu after 19 minutes. The chair umpire informed her that she was retiring because of back spasms. In Cincinnati Open Cincinnati Open, she withdrew shortly before the start of her first round match because of ongoing back problems and stated, "Unfortunately, my back isn't quite as good as it used to be."

The US Open, Williams had the seed of eighth. She played Maria Sharapova in the first round for the first time since the 2016 Australian Open, and she took the match straight sets, losing only one game per set. The second time she played, she beat Caty McNally with three sets. Third and Fourth rounds she beat Karolna Muchova as well as Petra Marti in straight games.

She was matched against an 18th-seed Wang Qiang in the quarterfinals which she beat just 45 minutes, losing only one game. Williams defeated fifth seeded Elina Svitolina during the semis to advance to the final in which she faced 15th seeded Bianca Andreescu for the second time in two weeks. Williams came back with a ferocious effort to draw the set five games each with Andreescu winning on the next set, by one 5-1 set. Williams was capable of breaking Andreescu's serve, and then take the match by straight set. Williams was playing her last match in the season match to finish the year as the top of the rankings. 10.

2020: AFTER The MATERNITY LEAVE, FIRST TITLE

Top seeded Williams won against Jessica Pegula in the 2020 ASB Classic final to claim her first singles win as mother of two. She along with Caroline Wozniacki advanced to the doubles finals in the tournament in which they fell against Asia Muhammad and Taylor Townsend. Through the 90s and 2000s the 2010s and the 2020s she was the very first female athlete in the professional era to win at minimum one title in the four decades between.

In 2020, the Australian Open was Williams' next tournament in which Williams was seeded 8th. She took single sets over Anastasia Potapova and Tamara Zidanek in the first and second rounds respectively, but lost in three sets in the third round to Wang Qiang in the third.

Williams began in the Top Seed Open as the top seed at the time that she was on the court when the WTA Tour resumed after a break caused by COVID-19. Williams took on their sister Venus to play their 32nd WTA game in round two following an exhausting three-set win over Bernarda Pera, who was eliminated in the first round.

After losing the first match, Williams prevailed. Williams was then beaten by his fellow American Shelby Rogers in the quarterfinals. Williams received a bye the opening round in the Cincinnati Open in New York and defeated Arantxa Rus at the end of the 2nd round and lost in the third round to Maria Sakkari in the third round, losing in three sets.

In the second major tournament of the year in 2020, the US Open, Williams was placed third. Williams beat Sloane Stephens in the third round of the event in three sets following her victory in the first two games with straight sets. Williams apologized for her loss in the match against Sakkari during the match for third place of the 4th round. Williams defeated Bulgarian Tsvetana Pironkova who was playing in her first event since having her baby three years before in the quarterfinals.

She took three sets over Victoria Azarenka before moving on to the semifinals. The match of her with Azarenka became the first encounter match between mothers in the Grand Slam semifinal. She also became the first athlete to make it into semifinals at the US Open and Grand Slam semifinals over four decades: between the years 1990, 2000s in the decade of 2010, and the year 2020.

In the delayed 2021 French Open, which was held in the chilly, rainy month of October Williams received the seed of sixth. Williams pulled out of the second match of her round against the wildcard Tsvetana Pironkova in reference to an injury to her Achilles she suffered during her semi-final defeat in the semi-finals to Azarenka during the US Open. Williams was beaten by Kristie Ahn with straight sets during the first round. Serena consequently did not make it to her place in the Grand Slam final for the first time since 2006 as a because of this.

2021: NOT PART OF THE TOP 40. AUSTRALIAN OPEN SEMIFINAL

Williams participated in The Yarra Valley Classic in the first week of the year, but she was forced to withdraw from the event prior to her quarterfinal game against the top seed Ashleigh Barty because of an injury to her right shoulder.

Williams 10, the 10th seed in the Australian Open, advanced past the second seed, Simona Halep, and the seventh seed, Aryna Sabalenka, before losing to the four-seed, Naomi Osaka, in the semifinals. They hadn't played each other in a major tournament since the tense final of the 2018 US Open final until Williams met with Osaka. Williams did a more lengthy than usual bow to the crowd when her departure from the tennis court following defeating Osaka during the Australian Open. Williams was asked whether or not she would be retiring from tennis in the press conference after the game. I would not tell anyone if I ever say goodbye as she said.

Serena Williams played her 1000th match of her career during the Italian Open. The second time around, Williams lost with ease against Nadia Podoroska.

Williams suffered an injury on the 29th of June while competing against Belarusian player Aliaksandra Svasnovich in the opening round of Wimbledon. This caused her to pull out of the match.

A leg injury forced Williams to pull out of this year's US Open in August. Williams's withdrawal led her to drop 19 spots to rank 41st in the world ranking, her lowest ranking at the year's end in 15 years.

2022 KING Richard is promoted and resigns, as well as attending WIMBLEDON and EASTBOURNE.

Williams has announced on December 20, 2021, that she would not be playing for her 2022 Australian Open due to the same problem with her leg. She was rated 241st by March 2022.

Together with her sisters with her sisters, she spent a large portion of the first quarter of 2022 promoting the story about King Richard her father. She appeared at a variety of awards shows, including the 94th Academy Awards.

In the 2022 Eastbourne International, Williams and Ons Jabeur made their return to competition in professional level. The team beat Shuko Aoyama as well as Chan Hao-ching during round one in round one and Sara Sorribes Tormo and Marie Bouzkova in round two. The pair then retracted from the event due to injuries sustained by Jabeur. Williams took a wildcard to the singles tournament during the 2022 Wimbledon Championships after her singles ranking dropped to 1204th.

The longest match in the tournament to date, which lasted more than three hours her opponent was Harmony Tan in the opening round.

Williams revealed her decision in an august Vogue piece that she was planning to "evolve from" from tennis following her participation in the US Open. It was a code word for retirement. Williams began her final games with a particular rank to be eligible for her 2022 Canadian Open.

Prior to falling to Belinda Bencic, she defeated Nuria Parrizas Daz in straight sets to win her first win in singles in the span of 14 months. Williams later played at her 2022 Cincinnati Masters, where she was defeated by the winner of the 2021 US Open, Emma Raducanu in the first round.

Williams announced prior to the tournament that it could be their last tournament together. She also said she'd be playing doubles against Venus again for the first time since 2018. This marked the very first time that a first-round doubles game during the U.S. Open at Arthur Ashe Stadium was the main event of Primetime. The team was defeated by Czech team consisting of Linda Noskova and Lucie Hradecka in the first round.

Chapter 4: Match Controversies

REPORTS ON MATCH-FIXING

Rumors of match-rigging started to surface as both Williams sisters made it to the top 10 and began to compete against each other at tournaments. In speaking about 2000's Wimbledon quarterfinal match between and the sisters, John McEnroe stated "Serena could not be allowed to prevail. Maybe Richard Williams can provide a speak regarding this." Elena Dementieva said in a post-match interview that Richard Williams dictated the outcomes of the games between the sisters in 2001, following their defeat against Venus at the Indian Wells semi-finals.

A few days later, Venus Williams abruptly withdrew from her semi-final game against Serena Williams at Indian Wells because of tendinitis. The incident led to a significant amount of speculation by the media and a number of fans demanded reimbursement.

BOYCOTT of INDIAN WELLS

The following week, at the 2002 Ericsson Open, Richard Williams claimed that the spectators were making racial comments to Williams. The event's director refused to offer an apology to Williams for the way he was treated.

So, neither of the sisters participated in the tournament despite the fact it was declared mandatory in the WTA circuit from the year 2009. Williams took the decision to compete after the 14-year-long boycott.

US OPEN OF 2004

An error was made by the chair umpire Mariana Alves during Venus Williams' US Open quarterfinal match against Jennifer Capriati; a video review confirmed that Williams shot was within bounds. In the third set of the match, incorrect line calls were made when testing the new equipment.

During the match, Williams challenged the chair in a couple of calls however he failed. Serena acknowledged that the victory of Capriati in the game was largely due to her 57 mistakes that were unforced however she also said that she accused Alves of having a mental breakdown and stated she "felt betrayed." Capriati made it clear in an interview after the match that she's also been victimized by poor decisions earlier in her career.

Alves did not officiate during the duration of the event Contrary to what many believe the fact that she did not officiate was not a reprimand since she was not required to. The debate rekindled calls to use technologies such as MacCAM and Hawk-Eye. MacCAM or Hawk-Eye systems and it was recognized as the reason for this.

US Open 2009

Williams struck her racket into the floor in her US Open semifinal match against Kim Clijsters after dropping the first set. She was issued a warning and could be penalized one point for an additional violation. Williams had her second serve declared a foot-related fault which gave Clijsters 2 match points while she was in the midst of losing between 4-6, 5-6 and 15-30. Williams angered the lineswoman who made the call and was yelling with her racket, and threatened to smash tennis balls down the lineswoman's neck if they did not slow down.

A camera on TV captured Williams talking to the lineswoman in the subsequent court meeting that involved the chair umpire, linewoman US Open officials, and Williams "I have never said that I would kill you. Are you truly real?" Because of the earlier warning of racket abuse and following incident Williams got a point-penalty for unsportsmanlike conduct and resulted the Clijsters beating Williams 6-4, 7-5. 7-5, 6-4. Williams was awarded the maximum of $10,000 on-site penalty (with another $500 penalty for racket abuse) the next day.

In November 2009 In November 2009, The Grand Slam Committee penalized her $175,000, but did not exclude herself from competing in the US Open or other Grand Slam competitions following further investigation. They also put her on a two-year suspension which stipulated that she would lose the right to participate at the next US Open if she committed an additional infraction during an Grand Slam tournament in those two years.

But, if she didn't commit any offenses over the next two years the penalty would be $82,500. Williams initially refused to offer the apology she needed for her behavior during the news conference she attended after the match, and also in a formal declaration that was released the following day. In the end, she expressed her regret, stating "I simply wanted to apologize since I'm quite proud and also a very emotional person and an extremely emotional person," and adding that "I would like to extend my sincere apologies for anyone I might caused offence to." She said that the incident has made her more humble.

US OPEN 2011

Williams called out "Come to the court!" when Samantha Stosur attempted to return the forehand Williams believed was an ace in 2011. US Open final.

In accordance with ITF's intentional hindrance rules, which says that "If an athlete commits an action that hinders another when he makes a stroke in the event that this is deliberate, he'll be disqualified from the match or when it is not voluntary the point will be replayed." The chair referee Eva Asderaki awarded the point to Stosur. Williams served was 30-40 when the penalty was imposed which gave Stosur the break to serve. Following the switchover Williams was furious with the umpire, and displayed a variety of unfavorable actions and remarks about her, such as warning Asderaki to the umpire that she needs to "look away" in the event that she saw Serena coming towards her.

After an error, Williams gained momentum in the opening set before getting back on track in the following game, but eventually was exhausted and lost the match 2-6 3-4. She did not offer Asderaki her traditional shake following the match. Williams placed second in the contest and mentioned the incident during her post-match comments "I did a great swing, but it wasn't worth the effort, "I added, adding that it wasn't crucial at the final.

Sam did an excellent job." Williams isn't believed to have used foul language in speaking to Asderaki during the game as per one ESPN writer, so she could not have violated regulations of "probation" that she placed on following her incident in 2009. Williams was eventually given a fine of $2,000 but was permitted to participate at the 2012 US Open because "Williams's conduct was verbally abusive but was not at the point of being a serious violation of the Grand Slam code of conduct," according to the decision.

US OPEN 2018

Williams' US Open performance in 2018 reached an unpopular conclusion when she fell in straight sets to Naomi Osaka in straight sets after being penalized for a game during the 2nd set in the final match. Williams was penalized for a code violation in the second set after Coach Patrick Mouratoglou, offered her coaching signals.

Williams was furious over the incident and demanded an apology form the chair umpire Carlos Ramos, alleging that her coach was just giving her thumbs up. Then,

Mouratoglou acknowledged that he was coaching. Williams was penalized with an amount of points for her third offense and that was smashing her racket into the court. Williams was penalized for a game for verbally assaulting an umpire 3 times during a row.

Williams asserted that the umpire been unfairly treated since she is a female. Williams received a total sanction of $17,000. Of this, $4000 was assessed as infractions to the rules of coaching as well as $3,000 for racket-related abuse, as well as $10,000 for abuse of words directed towards the umpire.

Other issues

In the early days of Williams's professional life, Williams's Williams sisters' hairstyles attracted attention from experts like Chris Evert and John McEnroe. Mary Carillo described the Williams sisters hair to be "noisy as well as disruptive." The beads would break and fell over the court. Particularly when it comes to a sport that is predominantly white, where the Williams sisters look and especially their body are often talked about as a scholar Nancy E. Spencer said that the comments made in opposition to the hairstyles that the girls wore traditionally resulted in "other" their sisters.

The first time in history they Williams sisters faced each other in the Grand Slam Tournament semifinal match at Wimbledon in 2000. After Venus's victory in straight sets, rumors regarding the possibility that Richard Williams rigged the contest began to surface.

When Venus pulled out of her scheduled quarterfinal match with the sister of her at Indian Wells in 2001, the concerns increased. Williams was constantly slammed by fans throughout an Indian Wells championship match two days after. Richard Williams said that a dozen people yelled racist epithets towards him and his daughter as they went to the stadium to support Williams in the finals with one person shouting "skin the guy alive." The Williams sisters stayed away from Indian Wells following this game till Serena and Venus returned in the years 2015 and 2016 respectively.

In the wake of the controversy surrounding Williams and Osaka's clash in the US Open final in the year 2018, US Open final, the Herald Sun in Melbourne published cartoons created by Mark Knight showing Williams throwing an argument throwing her tennis racket, while the umpire pleads with Osaka to "just let her win."

The cartoon was criticized harshly for being racist and sexist particularly by J. K. Rowling, Alexis Ohanian, the co-founder of Reddit as well as Williams husband. The main issue was the way Williams was depicted as a fierce black woman with a wide mouth, exaggeratedly large lips and a wide, nose that was flat and a slender posture and also the way Osaka Williams' opponent was shown as half-Haitian and half-Japanese wearing blonde hair. The video and photos taken from last year's US Open women's final demonstrate that Osaka's natural black hair was actually blonde in the moment which shook off some of the concerns. Editorial director of The Herald Sun stated that the cartoon received no criticism from social media.

Knight has defended his work, saying that his satire did not address the issue of gender or race instead focusing on the sexy behavior of athletes. He immediately removed his Twitter account after the controversy to "protect his family and his friends."

On a live show in September of 2019, Romanian television personality Radu Banciu claimed, "Serena Williams looks precisely like one of the monkeys in the zoo , with the red and black asses." Banciu was sentenced to $1,875 in the court of Romania's National Council for Combating Discrimination for his comments.

Chapter 5: Dateting Historization

Although Serena Williams has frequently held the highest ranking in singles tennis for women but she doesn't have to be single. This list of men who have been with Serena Williams will tell you more about these lucky guys. This list of famous buddies who Serena Williams has may possibly be interesting to you.

You've come to the right location if you're looking for answers to "Who is the last person Serena Williams dated?" Or "Who do you think Serena Williams married to?" The list below includes the former boyfriends from Serena Williams along with details about each as well as their birth dates, and jobs. The guys are shapes and sizes however they have one thing they all have in the same way: Serena Williams has either engaged in sexual relations or dated with all of them. Do your best not to be jealous at the guys

Serena Williams has dated because it's not difficult to do so.

Serena Williams keeps her personal life private, and does not talk about her past relationships or relationship background. However, Serena Williams declared her wedding with Reddit Co-founder Alexis Ohanian on December 29 on the 29th of December, 2016. In at the Australian Open, Serena Williams announced that they were expecting a baby.

Who do we know about Serena Williams' ex-boyfriends? The list below addresses. This list addresses "With whom have Serena Williams reportedly dated?" Check out the list below of men Serena Williams has dated.

DIMITRI DIMITROV
The year 2012 was the time Serena along with fellow tennis star Grigor Dimitrov are believed to have been in a relationship.
Age: 31
Birthplace: Bulgaria, Haskovo

EMORY STOUDEMIRE

Amar'e Stoudemire, an NBA player, was with Serena on her 2010 tour with Serena.

Amar'e Carsares Stoudemire, an American professional basketball player from Israel who recently played in the Israeli Premier League with Hapoel Jerusalem in the Israeli Premier League as well as in the Basketball Champions League, was born on the 16th of November 1982.

The Phoenix Suns, who took the ninth selection during the NBA draft in 2002, awarded him an NBA Rookie of the Year Award in 2003. He was a part of the NBA All-Star Game six times and was also selected five times as a member of be on the All-NBA Team, including a first-team choice in 2007.

After completing his education at Cypress Creek High School in Orlando, Florida, where he previously played basketball at five different institutions, Stoudemire entered the NBA draft as a pre-pro. He was awarded a variety of pre-season awards such as Orlando's Mr. Basketball. The highly athletic Stoudemire had an operation to repair microfractures on the knees as a result of chronic knee problems that affected him throughout his career. Prior to ending his time in the NBA in 2016, he was a player playing for his former team the Suns, New York Knicks, Dallas Mavericks, and Miami Heat. In the 2004 Olympic Games, Stoudemire was awarded a bronze medal by his US nation's team.

His extracurricular activities include performing, clothing label and record label, and a line of children's books published by Scholastic Press. Furthermore, Stoudemire has a large stake in Hapoel Jerusalem, the group which helped him win the award in the year 2017.

Age: 39

The place of birth: Florida, Lake Wales

OHANIAN, ALEXIS

Serena announced the announcement of her wedding with Reddit co-founder Alexis Ohanian public on December 29th, 2016. Reddit is a social news site. Reddit was founded by Alexis Kerry Ohanian. He is the chairman of the business as well as an American online businessman.

He also co-founded Initialized Capital, helped Hipmunk take off, and then founded Breadpig. He was a part of at the Howard High School class graduation in Maryland and delivered the graduation speech.

Serena along with him initially were introduced in May of 2015 in the Cavalieri Hotel in Rome. He initially chose to share a table with Serena and her friends who were extremely annoyed by her. She was able to recall telling the man, "We just don't want you to sit there" in an Vanity Fair interview. We'll use the table.

Then, after they became more comfortable and had a better

understanding of each other, they met for the first date of their lives in Paris shortly prior to her participation at the French Open. They explored the city for about six hours. Despite Serena's reluctance to commemorate birthdays she did make the exception, and she greeted him on FaceTime.

A few weeks prior to the time the proposal to Serena, the couple took time to go to Disney World. On the 10th of December in 2016, he recreated their first encounter at Cavalieri Hotel. Cavalieri Hotel by reserving identical rooms, cleaning out the pool in addition to making sure that he reserve the same table at which He sat with Serena in the beginning for the first time. He began to tell the tale of how they met before getting to one knee and asking the question.

The news was made public in April, 2017 that the couple was expecting their first child. They're still moving to different regions, but they will remain in the same house when she is born.

The couple got were married in November of 2017 and welcomed one daughter in September of the same year.

Co-founder and co-founders of Reddit.

Age: 33

The place of birth: New York City, New York

Chapter 6: 20 Outstanding Secrets About Serena Williams

After playing in the U.S. Open, Serena Williams, who has been a 22-time Grand Slam champion, announced her retirement. Williams is the one with had the greatest number of Grand Slam victories during the Open time period and is one short of the record held by Margaret Court, is coming to an emotional end.

Williams her career is set to come to an end in this year's tournament just 23 years after she won her first Grand Slam at the 1999 U.S. Open when she was just 17.

1. Her first tennis coaches was her father, Richard Williams and Oracene Price. The family moved from Compton, California, when Serena was born on the 26th of September 1981 located in Saginaw, Michigan, and Richard began instructing

her as well as her sister Venus the game in Compton, California. The two girls were taught at their home. Richard relocated the family members to West Palm Beach, Florida just a few years after Serena first took up a racket, so that his younger girls could join the tennis program.

2. "Tennis is a constant throughout my life, up to today. I think I picked up tennis even before my father claimed--when I was only 3 years old. young. I can't be more than 18 months old in the image of Venus pushing me around in an infant stroller on the tennis court.

3. Serena has skipped six years of playing in the junior tournament unlike many young tennis players that want to compete professionally. Richard has said in numerous interviews that he puts his daughters on the right track to their education to allow them to grow into young women , and most importantly, to shield their from the racism they'd likely encounter when they enter the world of

sports. Richard as well as Price often heard racial comments from parents and other spectators as they watched their daughters play in the seats. The parents of Serena wanted her to stay off until she reached the age of 16 to compete on the circuit. However, in 1995, just after her 15th birthday, she participated as a wildcard in Québec's Bell Challenge.

4. in 1997 Williams took on seventh-ranked Mary Pierce 7-6, 6-3 (7-3) in order to secure her first professional victory and progress into the Ameritech Cup semifinals, which took place in Chicago. Williams, who was 16 years old, was able to make historical records when, following the defeat of Pierce she pulled off an even bigger surprise by beating Monica Seles, who was ranked at the top of the list. 4.

5. Williams her eleventh and twelveth professional match put her in the books of sports history. Williams made Open historical records by becoming the player with the lowest ranking to beat multiple

top-10 players during the same event. Williams went from No. 99 on the global rankings following the conclusion of the year.

6. It was 1998 and the Australian Open was Williams' debut appearance at the top of an Grand Slam competition. In addition, it was the first match she played professionally ever played with her sister. In the second match of their series, Venus defeated Serena 7-6 (7-4) and 6-1.

7. Serena along with her twin sister were both winners of Women's Tennis Association competitions later the same year. Serena and Venus took home the doubles championship during the 1998 IGA Tennis Classic in Oklahoma City and became the third group of sisters to prevail in an event final.

8. Former champions such as Kim Clijsters, Conchita Martnez, Seles, and defending U.S. Open champion Lindsay Davenport made up the team that helped Serena win

her first Grand Slam championship. Serena's last challenge in 1999's U.S. Open final was defeated by the world's No. one Martina Hingis, 6-3, 7-6. (7-4).

9. A Black woman has won in a Singles Grand Slam match for just two times in history. The first time was Althea Gibson, in 1958. However, Serena wasn't done with her tennis career, as she and Venus were once again teaming together to take home in the U.S. Open doubles championship.

10. In the wake of allegations that Venus had to withdraw from the event to protect the attention of her younger sister. Serena received a scathing boo during the final match against Clijsters in the presence of her supporters from home at Indian Wells. Venus pulled out because of a knee injury prior to the time the match was scheduled to begin. Following Russian athlete Elena Dementieva claimed that Richard Williams had interfered with matches played by her daughter initial news was circulated.

Although Serena took home her second title during Indian Wells by defeating Clijsters in three sets, the entire family was cheered on during the ceremony to present the trophy through. This meant that Serena was unable to attend the tournament for more than 10 years up to 2015, and Venus returned following year.

An interview was conducted with Will Smith for "Red Table Talk,"" Serena noted, "Even when I came back 14 years later, it was absolutely difficult." "Discuss anxiety or post-traumatic stress disorder. I still can picture myself in the bathroom wondering, "Wait, I'm not returning." In simple terms I don't think I'm not supposed to. What happens if they boo one more? It was quite difficult.

11. Congratulations for completing your Serena Slam, which included victory at the 2002 U.S. Open, 2002 French Open, 2002 Wimbledon in 2003, and the 2002 Australian Open. If there were an

important turning point during Serena's time then it would be during this period. It's a bit ironic considering how successful she's had over the last two decades.

12. Serena and Venus have won the lifetime Golden Slam in women's doubles at the beginning of their careers, having won both the 2000 Olympics gold medal as along with the 1999 French Open, 1999 U.S. Open and 2000 Wimbledon as well as 2001 Australian Open titles. The first time in the history of tennis that players completed the Golden Slam in both the doubles and singles tournaments after Serena was awarded her first Olympic silver medal for singles in the 2012 London Olympics.

With 14 titles, Serena and Venus are unbeaten on the court in Grand Slam doubles finals.

14. As of 2009 Serena along with Venus made history as the only Black ladies within NFL the history of football to hold a

stake in the team after they purchased an 0.05 percent stake within the Miami Dolphins.

15. Serena was in the process of winning her Calendar Slam going into the 2015 U.S. Open, a feat that was only done in the past by 5 other players from the history of tennis. Don Budge (1937), Maureen Connolly Brinker (1953), Rod Laver (1962 and 1969), Margaret Court (1970) as well as Steffi Graf are her forerunners in this accomplishment (1988). Graf put an end to Seles in his plans to follow his example with a win in 1992 and 1991 by winning wins at Wimbledon.

While Graf took the title in the final three rounds in the Grand Slam that year, Seles got revenge after taking in 1993 the Australian Open and prevented Graf from repeating her feat. Serena was the closest to joining the elite club in 2015 however she was knocked out by a shock defeat in her U.S. Open quarterfinals by the unranked Italian Roberta Vinci and fell to the Italian in three sets.

16. Serena was discussing investing that she's been involved in for over 10 years, when she got married to the man she was married to, Reddit co-founder Alexis Ohanian. This is one of the many options she's planning on exploring when she gets rid of your tennis tennis racket. Serena said, "I've always been interested in technology, and I am fascinated by how technology can alter our lives. "That is the initial topic we talked about the first time I met my husband. It was the first time we connected. I was talking about investing.

17. It was unclear at the time Serena was pregnant for eight weeks with Olympia at the time she won in the 2017, Australian Open, her final Grand Slam title to date.

Some say I'm not the best player in the world, as I've never beat Margaret Court's record of 24 grand slam wins that she won before the beginning in the "Open era" in 1968. If I said I didn't wish to break to break that record you're lying. Yes, I do. But, I don't consider her on a regular basis. Yes, I think about this record when I'm playing competing in the Grand Slam final. Maybe I considered it too much which did not help.

My opinion is that I should have gotten over 30 Grand Slams. I had my opportunities after coming back after delivering baby. I had a C section, an embolism in my lungs again, and finally, I took home the Grand Slam. I enjoyed myself during my nursing. I used music to fight postpartum depression. However, I wasn't able to make it. Would, could maybe, and I may not look as good as I should have. However, it's not a problem since I've been there 23 times. It's amazing, actually. In the present when I must choose between raising my children and advancing my tennis game I'll go with the latter.

18. As a player in active play, Serena holds the most major championships, winning

39 awards in singles (23) doubles (14) and mixed doubles (two) divisions. Williams has won 73 singles titlesas well as 23 doubles titles as well as 3 Olympic gold medals and many more. Serena has the world record of most females' prize money ever with $94,524,403.

19. Serena's venture capital company, Serena Ventures, states that 76 percent of founding members of the portfolio businesses come members of "historically unrepresented communities" and that it obtained $111 million from its first round of capital.

20. In addition to managing Serena Ventures, Serena also operates her own clothing company, S by Serena, is on the Poshmark board and in 2021, she announced a collaboration in 2021 with Amazon Studios to create future docuseries.

Many of us will remember the day that Serena put on her famous catsuit return on at the Grand Slam stage at the 2019 French Open, which the French Tennis Federation later banned. In addition to the style of her black Nike outfit, Serena's health was considered in the design of the suit. The compression garment for the entire body was created to prevent blood clots as she suffered from this issue before. Serena had to battle an embolism in her lungs even when she was expecting Olympia.

She said in 2011 she had been told in 2011 "they informed me that I had numerous blood clots on both lungs." "Many people are killed as a result of the clots.

"My blood clots brought me many problems in addition, God, I haven't been able to count how many I have had in the past 12 months. This means that it's got some function. I've been wearing pants often when playing to ensure an adequate blood circulation. I'm able to play with no problems because it's an enjoyable clothes that serve the purpose of.

Chapter 7: Serena's Most Popular Rivals

In light of the numerous instances Serena played her older twin sister Venus during the semi-finals at Grand Slam events that was described in the preceding chapter, there's nothing to add. The thing that must be kept in mind is that they elevated the sport of tennis for women with respect to both the public image and performance to a new standard.

It's not easy to classify it as "rivalry" or "rivalry" since there is no animosity. After a few years it is not a good idea sense for "good copies" to result in one of their games. The initial combination of genuine interest and a shaky play when the sisters played against one another were key to their play. In many ways, it was an original act, considering there was only one other sister group in tennis is Bryan brothers. Bryan Brothers, who only play doubles.

It was only after Venus's tennis career caught fire, as did Serena's a few days later began to see the world begin to accept their talents. After their father Richard began to let girls play together on court, as and the girls making it a habit to praise their opponent's game in the context on the competition, that's the moment it began to take off in the minds of the public.

The most memorable time of their rivalry was between 2001 and 2003 when they played for the grand finals in six of their grand Slams and five consecutively from 2002-03in seven head-to head meetings.420 In the "Serena Slam" was at the expense of her sister, who didn't have a chance to beat she played in one of the four finals.

However, the handful of victories Venus has earned have come with a gruelling pace. She hasn't defeated Serena with a straight set in any head-to head match since she won her 2008 Wimbledon final.421 It also counts as the final of Venus Seven Grand Slam titles, and since that time, Serena has won 15 of her 23 Grand Slams, with the most notable being in 2009 the Wimbledon and the 2017 Australian Open finals over her older sister.

As Serena's run of success lasts for a generation, lots of her main rivals have the "if only" look to them as they were not able to sustain their success. Consider the example of Hingis who Williams has a 7-6 all-time advantage against.

Hingis Her rise to power was astonishmently fast. She became a professional in the year 1996, and won the Grand Slam doubles title at 15 at Wimbledon and became the youngest Grand Slam title winner the next season at the Australian Open en route to becoming the world's number. 1 player. Hingis has won 3 Grand Slam titles in 1997 but missed out on an opportunity to play in a calendar Slam just by being defeated by Iva Majoli during the semi-finals at the French Open.

At the time she lost in the final to Serena Williams in the 1999 U.S. Open final, she had already had won the number of Grand Slam singles titles, and there was plenty of evidence to suggest that she was leading tennis for women with Williams, the Williams siblings, Davenport, Pierce, and a revitalized Capriati. But the power that Williams introduced to women's tennis was something that Hingis did not really catch up to despite her impressive all-round game.

Then, injuries caused a lot of pain. Two ankle surgeries following her participation in the 2002 Australian Open final in which she lost four match points and fell to Capriati made her decide to pull out. Although she was able to make a brief comeback in 2005 and in 2006, it was never at the level required to compete with Williams.

Williams and Hingis have played just one other final , aside from their final at the 1999 U.S. Open, the 2000 Canadian Masters in which Serena was forced to retire after the final set because of an injury to her knee. Williams was victorious in the last three matches between the two, including a 2001 U.S. Open semifinal.422

Capriati was among the pioneers of powerful players that was expected to transform the sport with Graf as well as Seles. A lot of attention was paid to her first appearance in the WTA Tour at the age of 14 and the highs that followed her winning the Olympic silver medal when she was age 16 and her demise after her arrests on charges of shoplifting, as well as drug possession.423

The battle that came after Capriati's return to the sport was well-balanced, as Williams took 10 wins from 17 games. Capriati was the winner of all of his first 5 matches, winning both the Roland Garros and Wimbledon in the midst of a period where Williams was learning the skills was required to win Grand Slam titles.424 Capriati, in actual fact, is only one player to have ahead of Williams in grand championships. He won four out of their seven encounters at these tournaments. They have never played in the Grand Slam final, with six of the matches coming in the quarterfinals, and their only appearance in the semifinals was one-set win in the semifinals by Williams at 2003's French Open semifinals.425

The previous meeting which was won of Capriati at the 2004 U.S. Open quarterfinals, also included the line calls made against Williams which were so terrible the USTA Official Arlen Kantarian contacted him the next the next day apologize.426 The game ended in being one of the triggers for video review of serves, as well as the introduction of robotic cameras like HawkEye for both WTA as well as the ATP tours.

A tight rivalry that might be considered a special kind of one that could have continued for at the very least a decade if she hadn't decided to start a family. be a battle against Henin. Williams holds a 10-point advantage in the all-time series although it was shattered in the two and a half years since Henin quit his WTA Tour. Seven-time Grand Slam winner won three consecutive French Open titles and may be the only player, aside from her sister who was the one who gave Williams the fits due to the fact that Henin was arguably the best backhand for women's tennis during the 2000s.

The two players split the six Grand Slam matches across all four majors, with Williams winning the sole final in the respective tournaments, which was The 2010 Australian Open. While Henin will be remembered for his win at the 2002 French Open and the subsequent revenge match Williams won at Wimbledon in the same month, Henin also beat Williams in three majors in 2007: three majors - the French Open, Wimbledon, and the U.S. Open.427

She became a foe to Williams the power player through the spin she apply to her backhand, as well as frequent changes to her game plan for keeping her from balance "trying to exert more pressure on her hands, using heavier ball ... Try to play deep and force her back."

"I tried to alter the rhythm, as well as trying to get to the net, then slice a bit, and it assisted," she added. "Sometimes that worked. However, but sometimes it wasn't enough , because the problem for Serena is the fact that mentally she is able to play her best moments in crucial moments."428

These have been the tennis players that have gotten the most out of Williams throughout the years but there are also a few players who have given numerous chances to beat her through the years , but without much results.

On top of that list is Sharapova her loss streak against Williams is now twelve years and 18 matches after winning at the 2004 WTA Championships. Williams has stopped the Sharapova's Grand Slam bids during that period, and twice in tennis's Australian Open finals (2007, 2016) as well as the final of the 2013 French Open final.429

What fueled this unbalanced rivalry was a 2013 Rolling Stone profile on Serena which included what was considered to be her uncompromising criticism of Sharapova's private life as she talked to Venus over the phone which included Serena commenting that "She starts every interview by saying "I'm so glad. I'm very lucky' it's just boring. The girl will not get invited to fancy parties. But hey, if she's interested in being with the guy with the black eyes, then go for it."430

The writer of the piece implied that the "guy" who was in question was Grigor Dimitrov. one of the players Serena Williams was rumored to have had a relationship with prior to Sharapova. The article was published in the time frame between tennis tournaments like the French Open and Wimbledon, and also provided enough information for nearly every newspaper including, in particular, every British tabloid to make headlines that were breath-taking ahead of the tennis tournament at the All England Club.

The story was published four days after it was published, and just two days before Wimbledon, Sharapova lit into Williams for her comments . She brought a lot of heat to the she-said", she-said "Mean Girls" fight that was being played in public.

"If she's looking to discuss regarding something private, perhaps she should speak about her relationship with her husband who was married but has divorced and has children," the Russian shot back, making reference to Mouratoglou.431

Sharapova was also critical of Williams remarks in the piece about an alleged rape that involved an assault on a girl who was 16 located in Steubenville, Ohio, and Williams immediately apologized to the girl's family members for the incident. On the next date, Williams said she apologized to Sharapova at the pre-tournament dinner party for players in which she said she "made the effort to contact Maria since she was accidentally implicated in the matter by an assumption that were made by the reporter."432

Although Williams is masterful over Azarenka isn't as impressive as her win over Sharapova What is what makes the Belorussian stick out in the sense that she's been matched against Williams more than 10 times over Grand Slam matches without getting an advantage. This accounts for almost the entirety of their 21 games in that Williams is the winner with 17.433

Azarenka is close with Williams and who recently made the switch to playing full-time following giving birth to a baby in December of 2016 she had to drop two U.S. Open finals to Williams in three sets. Five of the 10 Slam matches which include the final four, required the final set.434 This will surely be an interesting test to observe if the bond that comes with motherhood strengthens their bonds as they battle for titles once Williams returns.

Serena Williams' Personal Life

You've learned a lot regarding Serena Williams and the spectacular achievements she has achieved while reaching the top in the world of tennis. You've seen glimpses of her character and competitive spirit reflected in her victories and losses however, there are still numerous elements that make up the entire of Serena Williams. Serena Williams is much more than the twin sister of Venus Williams, both on and off the court.

There's plenty of life in her, and a bit of mischief, and as she moves forward into what could be the biggest year in her life, she will not pick the tennis racket for the remainder of 2017 the world is hers to take.

Like the majority of professional athletes, they're placed in the spotlight in order to serve as "role role models" for the future generation. Williams is no different. However, in addition to being a star in tennis, Williams is an aspiring fashion entrepreneur who has her own line of clothing that she sells on the Home Shopping Network.435 She also has her own foundations that are charitable which include her Serena Williams Fund and The Williams Sisters Fund, as and The Yetunde Price Resource Center.436

The competitive spirit and the toughness was instilled in them at a very young age when she and Venus trained on the rundown tennis courts that were located in Compton. Their father described the experience in some shocking detail in his autobiography. He wrote that he'd bring "busloads of children from local schools to Compton to line the courts as Venus and Serena played. I made the kids repeat to the entire language of curses in the English language, which included 'n'. -----.' they paid the kids to do it and instructed them to do their worst.'"437

It was never a playful spirit for Williams as a young child. In the Rolling Stone piece, she confesses to cheating during matches against Venus in her youth and worked with her to trim the older sister's braids.438 Then there's the girl that you see on court and who is the one to jump and dance following a victory in a tournament, and flash her huge smile, which has so many sponsors waiting to sign endorsement deals.

There would have been more of it throughout the years, were the dust-up at Indian Wells in 2001 not occurred. "The false accusations that our matches were rigged caused us to be cut, hurt and slashed us in a profound way," she wrote in the article in Time Magazine ahead of her 2015 return to India. "The subtext of racism was confusing, painful and inexplicably unfair. ..."I immediately felt unwelcome, unloved and afraid."439

This is a huge amount for a professional athlete to handle. There were also the physical issues she faced and her health, particularly when she was fighting depression following the death of her half sister Yetunde. There's no secret superpower she is a tennis player because Williams is a victim of the same body issues that every person has. Some could be exacerbated by the ease of assign various terms to 6-foot-1 Venus who is described as slim and graceful, as opposed to Serena's frame of 5 feet 9 inches, which is often referred to as "muscular" because it is the initial or as one of some of the initial adjectives.

"I needed to become comfortable with the fact I had weakness was weight." Serena said. "Especially being a child with Venus who's thin and tall and model-like, and my I have thick hips and all..

"I was once a girl and I wanted to become like her. I wanted to be thinner but I wasn't and I needed to accept that I'm likely to have bigger and bigger boobs. I'm likely to grow bigger and enjoy it. Therefore, I believe it's beneficial for many others who are curvy or more brash to feel confident about themselves."440

We're now looking at Serena's clothing collection, which is known as "ANERES." The line debuted in 2003, and then added an apparel collection later in the year. In contrast to her sibling Venus who is known for her sportswear, Serena opts for more casual attire. Soon after the debut of her business was partnered together with Blue Intimates for a lingerie collection.441

The partnership she has signed with Home Shopping Network gets the ANERES brand noticed by various groups, which is a part of the under-appreciated business acumen Williams has demonstrated. One of her achievements was her ability to use the an "see-now purchase-now" fashion show concept during the ever-popular New York

Fashion Week, that gave her a multi-media platform to showcase her line.442

Although dealing with racism has been an integral part of almost every aspect of Williams her life, she has also always been forefront of fighting sexism within her sport. In March of 2016, BNP Paribas tournament director Raymond Moore was rightfully blasted for his remarks about women's tennis. He claimed"the WTA "doesn't take decisions, and they're lucky," before going one huge step further and saying that "if I were a female tennis player, I'd lay down each night to my knees in prayer and thanks God Roger Federer and Rafa Nadal were born, as they've carried the sport. They truly have."443

The outcry was swift and total. Moore was forced to resign after the incident. However, it brought up the issue of pay disparities on one of the ATP as well as WTA Tours. In the U.S. Open was the first event to have equal compensation for prize winners in 1973. It was not until Wimbledon was the first to do so in 2007 for the of the four Grand Slam events to reach the milestone.444 Williams took the challenge to equal pay in a piece in Porter Magazine by calling out women to "break through many obstacles in their path towards success."

In the essay, she also stated that the topic about equal wages "frustrates me since I am aware that I too, as you have put in the same job and sacrifices like our male counterparts. I would never wish for my daughter to receive lesser than me to do the same job. I would not either. you."445

Women's empowerment can be seen in a variety of ways and in many places. She was awarded the Sports magazine's Sportsperson of the Year for 2015 despite not being able to participate in the calendar Slam and the cover photo of her sitting on an throne of gold with an lace black bodysuit and black pumps generated quite a stir. Sports Illustrated remarked that the cover image was "Serena's ideato show her personal ideals of femininity, strength and power."446

The reason for this decision by Sports Illustrated to give her the Sportsperson of the Year title was a similarly provocative decision that was more than the 3 Grand Slam titles and near an unprecedented year in the courts. According to the editor Christian Stone put it, "we have chosen to honor Serena Williams too for reasons that are in the greyer and less comfortable realm, where gender and race intersect with the games."447

In the article, Williams recounted just how difficult 2015 was for her physically. Her knee tendinitis and elbow pain that slowed her serve, as well as the 101-degree fever which put her at the brink of pulling out of her participation in the French Open final. She also remembered the moment when she mental shifts. A code violation by Sharapova like the one she was given at the time of her 2001 U.S. Open final was received with disdain before she went on to win the next point.448

The maturity of Williams was also apparent in the essay she wrote to mark the return of Williams to Indian Wells. She wrote three drafts and Williams her mother Oracene Price acknowledged that nobody wanted her to leave, stating that she wouldn't return if it weren't for her. "Not because I couldn't forget them, but because of my integrity. If they didn't think that I should be there? Don't I have a right to be there."449

Her father was the one who first saw her daughter's need for this trip after the tearful drive back home to Los Angeles after winning that title. Williams believed in her faith as a Jehovah's witness also played a role in her decision in her belief in her faith and the strength of forgiveness.450 This might be the main reason in her parents' perception of Williams as an adult woman and their daughter.

"To be able to forgive she has a problem with this," Price noted. "It's an enormous move for her. Because she's the type of person who's going to take revenge on you and that was not going to end."451

Then she utilized her fame and power to benefit others by launching a fundraising campaign in conjunction with The Equal Justice Initiative to coincide with her return. Williams has raised more than $200,000 by hosting a hit tennis session and souvenir racket as well as tickets to her first match at Indian Wells.452

It was a time she considers to be the best of her career. Strong words considering the an incredible 23 Grand Slam titles and countless other prizes won during an entire career that is nothing but unrivalled in the sport she plays.

"It let go of a lot of emotions that I didn't realize I felt," she said. "I was awestruck by how emotional I felt and how happy I felt when everything was done and done."453

Williams recognizes that her voice is standing out in the current time and age. She knows she needs to be more effective and be more. However, she is conscious of her role in this era and has taken online courses to gain knowledge about U.S. civil rights history and was disappointed by the amount of information she lacked.454 She has a hope that "if anyone hears me perhaps that person will be a voice and help. I'm embracing the idea. I'm ready and thrilled to be a part of the emerging movement,"455" is a term that is slowly gaining popularity in both sports and in the realm of pop culture.

In the final part of Williams her personal life is, perhaps, the most recent one which is her whirlwind romance with Alexis Ohanian. she will soon be his wife and the mother to their baby. The two had an unplanned meeting at a party in Rome in 2014 and slowly began dating.456

While Williams is always visible to the world Ohanian is no person who isn't averse to being in the spotlight. He is a king in the tech and internet business. He came of age at just 22 years old when He co-founded Reddit which has since grown to become one of the most popular news aggregation sites around the world.457 Ohanian would go on to develop various social media sites and an investment firm prior to the chance encounter in Rome.

Williams wrote about the day Ohanian proposed to her via poems on Reddit While Ohanian chose the more traditional way of posting a text message to his facebook page which said "She replied yes."458

Despite the general feeling to her happiness from both her family and friends in relation to her pregnancy and her upcoming wedding, there were people who were uncomfortable about the prospect of an interracial wedding. Former tennis star Ilie Nastase made a horrific (no pun intended) in this instance, off-color comment regarding Williams her pregnancy, and then responded to the question by saying "Let's look at the color it is. Chocolate and milk?"459 as the head of the Romanian Davis Cup team.

Williams was adamant about Nastase through an Instagram post, pointing out the bigger view that the "world has come a long way and yet there is many more miles to go."460 After that incident, a lot of Williams Instagram accounts have been those of a bubbly, expecting mom-to-be, who is getting ready for what is certain to be a new chapter in her life.

Chapter 8: The Legacy Of Serena Williams

While she still trails Margaret Court by one Grand Slam title, which is the most of female players of any time, it could be stated the following: Serena Williams is the greatest female tennis player of all time and one of the top players in tennis regardless of gender.

Serena and her sister revolutionized tennis with a power that was unmatched in the WTA Tour, which had only seen glimpses among the stars of the past with Evert, Navratilova, and Graf. Although many fans had hoped they would see enduring rivalries between Williams with the likes of Hingis, Capriati, Henin, Clijsters, and Sharapova it's not surprising that at the end of the day, the only other tennis player to have the endurance of Serena Was her sibling Venus.

The record-breaking 23 Grand Slam titles are a standard that will probably be unbeatable until long after Serena Williams' retirement. There are only two active players who are holding at minimum five titles titles: Venus Williams (7) and Sharapova (5). Although Sharapova has won her first record-breaking Grand Slam, Serena Williams has achieved it three times as the sole Open Era mark that is not within her reach is the seven Evert French Open titles.

Williams is absent due to her pregnancy, which is a sign that her legacy has a book or two left to write. While attempting to match and perhaps surpass Court's record of 24 Grand Slam titles is at the top of the list, she could create Open Era marks for most Wimbledon and U.S. Open titles. Williams will need two more titles at the all-England Club in order to be able to match Navratilova and her next tournament in Flushing Meadow will move her ahead of Evert in the race for the most. A win at Roland Garros will mean she is one of just four women who have at minimum 4 French Open championships, and her seven Australian Open singles titles are three more than her closest rival.

However, Williams her legacy on court isn't limited to her singles game. It is possible to write a complete section about her accomplishments as a doubles player with her sister. They've teamed up for fourteen Grand Slam titles, never losing a final in these tournaments. They are tied in second place with Gigi Fernandez as well as Natasha Zvereva, and is well ahead of the 21 titles won from Navratilova as well as Pam Shriver. One of the most successful runs that the Williams sisters experienced was between 2008 and 2010, where they won six out of their possibility of 8 Grand Slam titles as well as the gold medal at Beijing.

In fact, the power of the siblings to be a team when trying to outdo each other singles could have contributed to their endurance power. Who wants to quit when you can continue playing with your closest partner?

In addition, there is nobody better than Williams to complete those final chapters considering the impact that Mouratoglou's been able to have. Although there are rumors that the two having a romantic relationship soon after she became her coach are neither verified or disproved, 461 there is no doubt about the influence he's been instrumental in shaping the final stage of her career following his 2012 arrival.

Mouratoglou is the only tennis player Williams will pay attention to. And if the interview he did with L'Equipe is an indication, he'll be patient and cautious when getting her fit enough to increase the Grand Slam totals.

"She is leaving the doors unlocked ... the lady wanted to know if I could sit and wait for her. I need to think on it because it's a long time that's at most one year. I doubt she'll be able to return in the next Australian Open. We can see this with Azarenka that she isn't coming back prior to Wimbledon despite being eagerly anticipating. Returning at an appropriate level following previous experience like this isn't an easy task. She's able to achieve it."462

One aspect of her legacy which appears to be being consolidated in the fact that she's by far the most admired female athlete of African descent ever. This is partly due to the absence of heroes in every sport, but for tennis, the role models of African-Americans start in the form of U.S. Open pioneer Althea Gibson in the 1950s. There were Arthur Ashe on the men's side to admire In the time between Ashe's retirement as well as Williams becoming an adolescent, the most prominent tennis player of African descent was Zina Garrison who reached her first Wimbledon final as a singles player.

There were others who have been sports heroes Of course. Jackie-Joyner Kersee and Florence Griffith spring immediately to mind when we think of the 90s, and they were rightfully so. However, they were not visible and off the radar except every four years when they were able to compete for America. United States at the highest levels of track and field during the Olympics. Also, while Cheryl Miller was a standout basketball player but there was no national female basketball team within America while she was playing at the top of her game.

While she's not more outspoken than Williams, Lisa Leslie serves as a trailblazer for the other side in certain areas due to the fact that her career has coincided with the development of the WNBA that is now in its third decade of being professional sports. With tennis being an all-year-round sport, Williams has never truly gone under the radar thanks to her performance and her words. In today's society there's always a media cycle looking to get new information, or often, fresh controversy.

This is the place where Williams has done an amazing task of standing out from the crowd in her stance for equal pay for many more events, or how she reacted to Nastase's snarky remarks. The return of her essay back to Indian Wells proved to be a significant moment in her life, one that was more than tennis. In this essay,

Williams not just acknowledging that she was an ideal role model for children regardless of gender, religion however, her tone of voice demonstrated her willingness to accept the role of an African-American.

Additionally, Williams who is a businesswoman aids Williams the charitable philanthropist. The idea that was initially conceived in Ghana has since spread to other African countries , including Uganda, Kenya, and Zimbabwe.463 The school located in Kenya is now home to over 400 students, and is more than half female according to her requirements that the students must at least 40% female. The school has reached an exhilarating where two students from the school have earned the right to go to college, a first within the town of Wee.464

Her circle of friends has always consisted of celebrities, such as Martha Stewart and Facebook executive Sheryl Sandberg. Her fascination is unstoppable. The ANERES clothing line is a passion for her, but is almost a way to connect to her ever-growing circle of famous friends. It's not everyday that Vogue Editor Anna Wintour takes time out of her day to tweak your brand's clothing, however she did exactly that for Williams her debut New York Fashion Week show in 2015.465

Due to her upcoming wedding to Ohanian The circle will grow and could dramatically increase Williams foundations that support charities as well as international. With his technologically-savvy personality and his savvy use of technology, the message they create could be on the forefront of a brand new approach to doing things moving forward.

It will be people who will remember those Serena Williams moments of controversy first, whether it's the initial Indian Wells saga in 2001 and the iconic Puma catsuit she wore at her 2002 U.S. Open, the Nike leopard-print dress she wore to the U.S. Open466, or the U.S. Open466 or the threat made by the lineswoman during her 2009. U.S. Open. All things are right to be judged with the same rigor as the person's personal biases that they view them.

However, to evaluate each one of those aspects separately is a risk of not seeing the full image of what Serena Williams is. Whatever the status of fame or wealth, each human being is an intricate human being with emotion and vitality. Serena Williams is a tennis iconic figure, a pioneer of both her sport and race. She is a woman who is well-aware of the events that happen around her. She is also soon to become an aspiring mother and wife. She'll add her distinctive perspectives to the multi-colored world she has shown to the world for only 35 years.

If she does swing an instrument for over the course of 3.5 years, there's an opportunity that she could make a mark in society for another 35 years.

Chapter 9: Serana Retirement

"I have never been a fan of the term'retirement'" Williams composed. "Perhaps the most appropriate term to describe what I'm doing is advancement.' I'm here to inform you that I'm moving away from tennis and towards other things that mean much to me."

Williams who will turn 41 in a month Williams has 73 singles for vocation titles, 23 duplicates of profession titles, and greater than $94m in career rewards.

Williams is widely regarded by many as being among the top athletes ever. In her Vogue article, she noted that some of her critics argue the fact that she's not won the most epic homerun competitions in women's tennis history In any case.

"There are those who believe that I'm not the top GOAT player because I did not meet the record set by Margaret Court of her 24, which is huge homerun wins which she achieved prior to the "open time" that began the year 1968." Williams composed.

"I'd claim that I claimed that I didn't require that record."

She announced that she would resign following her participation in the U.S. Open, which will begin in the end of August until September. If she wins, it will tie her to Court's Huge record of home runs.

"I could not say whether I'm ready to take home New York. But, I'll try," Williams expounded on the contest that takes place in Sovereigns.

She has counted the sponsorships of various companies like Nike, Audemars Piguet, Away, Beats, Blunder, Gatorade, Gucci, Lincoln, Michelob, Nintendo, Wilson Outdoor supplies, and Procter and Bet.

Nike announced that it would continue cooperating with Williams. "Serena Williams was reclassified as an authentic hero. Her legacy goes beyond sport and has helped to accelerate the age of aging," the organization said. "We expect to continue our established and well-established organization alongside her. We also say thank you to her for everything she's done and will continue to do from here to the present."

Williams focused on her family members in the declaration, saying that her nearly five-year-old daughter should be a mature and experienced sister. Williams is married with Reedit the pioneer Alexis Ohanian.

"I have never had to be forced to choose between tennis or the family. I don't think that's right," Williams composed. "In the case that I were someone I would never write this, since I'd already be out playing and winning , while my spouse was working hard on the job of giving our loved ones a hug."

She also shared an Instagram post on Tuesday that read: "I need to zero into being a mom with my main goals, and finally discovering a different, but exhilarating Serena. I'll be savoring these next few weeks."

Professionally, she is hoping to expand Serena Adventures, a little venture firm of just six people that was perhaps the first financial investor in Masterclass. The company raised $111 million in external funds this year.

Williams wrote that only two percent of funds go to women, and "for us to make a difference there must be more people who look like me should be present, giving money in return."

Dominance that spans decades

Williams was a mere participant in two tournaments throughout 1999. She took home her the Grand Slam Cup in Munich in September. Williams scored her first professional win against her sister, who was a year older, in the finals, defeating Venus by three sets. Serena began quickly, holding her sister's advantage to three points over the first five games, while also winning her first match 6-1. Venus however, recovered to win the second set with the score of 6-3 before Serena recovered to earn her first victory in just four attempts for bragging rights.84

It's not like you could have imagined by watching Serena that she was awarded bragging rights following the match. In contrast to previous matches between the two, which frequently see both sisters fighting tensions with they fought over times it was a high-powered tennis match that exhausted both. It was clear it impacted Williams' younger sister. Williams.

"I'd never beat Venus and I wasn't aware of what it felt like," Serena said. "It's difficult to accept this win."85

The season ended in The Porsche Tennis Grand Prix the following week, where she lost the match to Testud with three sets during a round-of-16 match.86 However, Williams was younger. Williams received the honor of being named as the player with the highest improvement in the WTA Tour for the year and was the number. 4 player around the globe.

2000

Williams chose to participate at Williams chose to play in the Australian Open as her first event of the year. She was entered into Melbourne as the number. 3 seed. She was forced to adjust to the attention of her opponents instead of being capable of sneaking up on opponents being an outsider. Williams had to battle her way through wild card and local favourite Andrea Grahame in three sets in the opening round.87

Things resumed normal in the following two rounds, as Williams won straight sets against Nicole Pratt and Sabine Appelmans however, her fourth-round match against 16th seeded Likhovtseva was a complete disaster. Perhaps it was the insufficient match-fitness after having not played for over three months, or simply an unlucky playing day, Williams was awash with shots because her backhand was failing her, and she committed 32 unforced errors.88

She was leading 3-1 in the opening set, but Likhovtseva took eight consecutive wins that spanned both sets. Williams came back to draw the second set 3-3 however, the Russian came back to win the match.

"I didn't have the shots ... It was like I was unable to accomplish anything," Williams said. "There's no reason for me to be a loser in this game. I couldn't get my groove on throughout the entire match."89

She was back to Paris in the Open de Gaz as a champion for the first time. She was close to being winning, but fell by a straight set to the Tauziat team in the semi-final. This was enough for her to win her first title of the season with a win in Hanover, Germany, where she took home the Faber Grand Prix with an overwhelming 6-1, 6-1 win of Denisa Chladkova.90

There were high-profile tournaments that she had to compete within America. United States at both Indian Wells and Miami however Williams could not put together enough great performances both to win. She required three sets to beat the first of her two games in Indian Wells before beating Clijsters to reach the quarterfinals however, Pierce was far superior in the quarterfinals as Williams only took three games against the American players from France.

In Florida she was dismissed in the previous round in the tournament.

Capriati is currently enjoying an impressive professional and personal revival at the WTA Tour, eliminated her in three sets match.91

At her next event in the Amelia Island tournament Amelia Island, Williams was forced to withdraw after the first round in the second round against Argentina's Paola Suarez because of an injury to her knee. Williams was previously afflicted with tendinitis during this time in the past and the injury was found to be the same as this condition.92 Not putting her faith in this early stage in Williams' career Williams decided to stay clear of the clay-court season. This means that she would not play in any European tournaments nor French Open in 2000.

Following what turned out to the second time she had been laid off for three months within a calendar year Williams returned to the court at Wimbledon in which she was seeded eighth seed. Completely healthy in both physical and mental health Williams dominated the first five opponents she faced, not dropping a single set, and losing just 13 games over the 10 sets.

In the semifinals her sister, who was a year older, loomed. Venus Williams was still looking to win her very first Grand Slam singles title and was not in the final since she lost to Hingis in 1997's U.S. Open. The match brought back the talk about the Watson sisters' match during Wimbledon in 1884, as the chance to play in the Grand Slam final was at the line.

In terms of aesthetics, the game ended up being a complete disappointment because the sisters looked hesitant and shaky. They never got into a rhythm, however Serena Williams was overwhelmed by the moment and was throwing inconsistencies that she did not cause across the court. They both played the serve-and-volley sport that rewards players who are good at Wimbledon and they were willing to compete and beat one another from the baseline, however Williams was younger and Williams just couldn't get the ball in place.

The final score was 7-6, 6-2 (7-3) triumph for Williams' older brother, which was enough to leave Serena devastated after the match. After the match ended with her sixth double error and the younger Williams had a hysterical cry on the sideline and was crying during the post-match interview room.93

"I did not play very well today. It was not going well to me." she explained. "Venus performed quite well today, and she showed her best against me. I guess I wasn't prepared. I was expecting to be a lot better today. I set out to be better. I'm just 18 years old; Venus is 20. I have a lot of more years to go before me."94

The manner in which the game unfolded was also the first time in their lives that the sisters were enthralled by the possibility of "match-fixing" that was where the sisters, along alongside their father decided who would be the winner of a certain event. Richard Williams, who did not even participate in the game and was strolling around the streets surrounding the all-England club since the match was so tense was able to dismiss the notion as Venus offered a sharp, "No, not that I know of," response to the question.95

In the event that there were a bright side to this awful match there was one: the sisters won the third time they have won the singles Grand Slam title at Wimbledon by winning straight sets against Halard-Decugis as well as the Japanese Ai Sugiyama.

Serena Williams stayed away from tennis until the beginning of August, however, her sister, who was a dominant force, was dominating headlines and tournaments with wins at Stanford as well as San Diego. Her Williams's younger Williams came back to challenge her crown in Manhattan Beach, and for the duration of one tournament the whole thing clicked.

She was a breeze through the first two games and played hard throughout the third set she needed three sets to make the quarterfinals to the final. Williams defeated the No. fourth seed Conchita Martinez before getting past the top seeded Hingis in the semis. The final match against Davenport was a wild battle of erratic and brilliant tennis, as the two fought in the scorching heat as temperatures soared above 90 degrees.96 There was just 1 break during the opening set that Davenport took advantage of to take the match the set 6-4. They broke five times in the second set, as Williams played to a draw, and they broken each other's serves three times in the final third set. Williams took home the biggest break as she broke Davenport in love, who was trailing 6-5, to cause an end-of-match tiebreaker. After the two divided the first two points Williams took the last six points in the two-hour 28-minute game that saw 21 double faults committed by both players.97

The injury bug bitten Williams twice in 2000 and this time it was at the end match of the du Maurier Classic in Montreal. Williams was in a tie with Hingis by 3-0 during the 3rd set when she began complaining of discomfort within her left foot.98 The injury would not stop her from the fight for a second time to defend the U.S. Open title where Hingis would be again the top seed. Williams was seeded as fifth.

Similar to Wimbledon, Williams was impressive during the opening rounds winning four times without losing a single set, and getting challenged to a tiebreak only once during those eight sets. In the quarterfinals the second-ranked Davenport was able to avenge her defeat at Los Angeles with a thorough defeat of 6-4, 6-1 to Williams.

Davenport had only won one of the six previous matches between Williams and Davenport and she made use of the unconventional strategy of continuously hitting shots into a corner to make Williams to lose patience when she returned them.99 Also, she got an increase in confidence early in the match when she fought against three break point by Williams her impatience accelerated her defeat. Davenport took advantage of one break opportunity in the initial set and then exhausted Williams by forcing her to stop five matches, which was five-1 during the next.

"The different was that Lindsay simply played better than me," Williams said. "You cannot afford to be playing anything other than your best during the semifinals of the Grand Slam."100

She didn't qualify for singles in the Sydney Olympics due to the fact that Davenport as well as her sister were among the most highly ranked American players. However, she did join forces with Venus to take home gold in the women's doubles event, beating the Dutch team comprising Kristie Boogert, Miriam Oremans 6-1, 6-1. This brought their winning streak up to 22 games, and for Serena she was a cheerleader for her sibling as she took home the gold medal at singles just a day before.101

"It was a great moment for me on Wednesday, watching Venus triumph," Serena said. "It is the same type of feeling today."102

The younger Williams completed her year with a win at the Toyota Princess Cup in

Tokyo prior to when she and Venus were off for the remainder of the year to complete academic work.103 Overall it was a very successful year for Serena and she racked up the title of three and earned a rank of no. 6 though the decrease of two spots can be attributed to the fact that she did not play in events she took part in due to injuries.

2001

It was a remarkable rise of Williams to her firmly established Top 10 status, but getting to the top of the heap and making it into the top 5 in which her sister was residing proved to be a tough test. Williams was this time a participant in an event in Sydney to get ready for the Australian Open, and Hingis knocked her off into the quarterfinals.104

The same scenario could play out the same way in Melbourne in the finals as"Swiss Miss, "Swiss Miss" took revenge for the sting of her U.S. Open finals defeat by a tense three-set win. Hingis took the first set before Williams requested help from the trainer after she felt faint. After receiving fluids as well as "some pink substance" Williams said tasted "terrible," she roared back to win the next set.

In the third, it was awe-inspiring the third set was thrilling, with Williams leading 4-1, and then having Hingis take her down twice after bouncing off four break points that she had her own to even the match. Williams responded by breaking her own and was just two points away from putting the match by serving before Hingis was back to meet the challenge. She would ultimately take in the final set 8-6.105

Following the match, Williams claimed she had an upset stomach. She also said she had not eaten much in the two previous days, however Hingis did not buy any of that in her post-match interview.

"You didn't know if she was sick from food poisoning, or any other issue," said Hingis, who claimed her first set play was one of the best ever in her professional career. "She was running very well. If she was unable to finish in some of the rallies that were long, it was more because I had worn her out, and not the fact that anything else that could be the problem."106

There could be some truth in these words, considering that just an hour after losing, Williams was able to beat a triple-set doubles match alongside her twin sister. Another fact is that Williams didn't make herself any better by making 54 unforced errors , as opposed to only 29 errors made by Hingis.107

Williams didn't play again after Indian Wells, a tournament which will live on in tennis for women's the wrong reasons. It started off as normal that Williams placed seventh in the draw and navigating the court. Williams did not lose any of her first three matches , and defeated Davenport 6-1, 6-1 in the quarterfinals to set the stage for an opponent in the semifinals with her twin sister.

Following the time that Venus Williams had defeated Elena Dementieva in the quarterfinals of the tournament, the Russian was a bit sceptical during her post-match interview declaring that she believed Richard Williams had already determined the player who would go on into the semifinals. If asked directly if other players were of the same opinion Dementieva replied "no" and said that she "didn't discuss the issue with other players."108

While not explicitly stating that the match was rigged, Dementieva also felt that the 1999 final in Miami was a pre-planned outcome and said that "if you watched this game it was hilarious." This case the WTA was unable to assist by not making a subsequent statement in response in response to Dementieva's comments.109

The second issue occurred on during the semifinals, when Venus was forced to withdraw only minutes prior to the time scheduled for the match because of a knee injury. It is crucial to be aware of since players are required to provide at minimum 30 minutes' notice in order that officials of the tournament can change the order of play and other such. In the end the Tournament director Charlie Pasarell only learned of Venus withdrawing via the

PA system in the court. The words of his speech did not assist:

"I just wish she had taken the time to give it a shot. This is a huge blow to the sport of tennis more than an single tournament."110

This assertion, along with the way Richard Williams and the sisters have dealt with media with concerns about possible match-fixing, has sparked the public's interest. This time, The National Enquirer ran an article that claimed that two sources close Richard Williams had told Serena to be defeated by Venus during the Wimbledon final last year.111

In the following interviews, following the game that did not take place both sisters spoke out in a clear claim that the game was fixed as well as that father had pre-arranged any outcome to a game between the two. In fact, Serena added further controversy with her statement "I think that maybe if dad had made a decision, maybe Venus would not be leading 4-1. Perhaps it would be three-all in a few minutes from now."112

The next day following day, the WTA eventually issued an announcement that stated "they had been aware of claims being circulated about Venus as well as Serena Williams' head-to-head matches." But , they said that they did not find evidence of any wrongdoing, and the two players have denied all claims of any kind. assertions.113 But the haze of controversy of this entire affair continued to grow, and the situation got more pronounced the following day.

As Serena was practicing warm-ups to prepare for her final match fight against Clijsters the duo of Richard along with Venus Williams made their way to their seats. Though the media's accounts of members differ on certain points however, there was one thing that is consistent that both were cheered on by the crowd of more than 16,000. The cheers continued throughout the match and, at one point before the game began, Richard Williams shook his fist at the crowd.114

The match was not a physical assaults and the officials of the tournament did not record any racist abuse or threats directed at Richard or Venus although security was eventually there to watch them throughout the game which was taken in three sets by Serena with three sets.115

The main issue occurred after nine days, after the match, when Richard Williams told USA Today that "When Venus and I were sitting down I was constantly interrupted by people who said "n -----.' One of them said"I I wish it was 1975 and we'd smear you alive. I believe Indian Wells disgraced America."116

Pasarell was also mentioned in the article Pasarell was also quoted in that story, saying "I was crying when all this was happening. It was inhumane on the part of the audience to be able to do that."117

The sisters did their best to address the questions about racism that were being asked of them prior to their next event in Miami But remember that Venus was only 20 years old and Serena only 19. Venus tried to avoid the issue, however she did not forget that "Whatever occurred, it occurred. I'm not able to alter it. It's not something I could do to change it."118

Serena stated that her father didn't reveal the comments she said in USA Today and also said she believed it was more in her best interest since "maybe I'd have been less emotional over it."119 Two weeks after the incident began with some offhand remarks made by Dementieva she claimed at the press conference in Miami she believed "she was lying" and "didn't believe" that it would get to the amount of scrutiny.120

In the final phase the sisters would begin to boycott Indian Wells, which would continue until Serena returned to the sport in 2015. By 2009, the Indian Wells event was one of the four events that were Premier Mandatory in the WTA Tour that eligible players were required to attend. The tour also stated that a failure to attend such events could result in a suspension if the player participated in promotional activities to promote the event missed.121 There could or may not have been a set distance of one hundred miles as the break-off point , since the Williams sisters were located 128 miles away from Indian Wells.122

Williams tried her best to avoid the distractions Indian Wells created, but she was beaten by Capriati during the quarterfinals at Miami. Williams didn't play again up until the French Open, where Capriati's revival continued with a three-set victory against Williams during the semifinals.123 At one time, she was the icon and warning for teens in tennis for women, but now a mature 21-year-old, Capriati would go on to win the victory of Roland Garros and rally to beat Williams again in Wimbledon in the quarterfinals.

www.ingramcontent.com/pod-product-compliance
Lightning Source LLC
Chambersburg PA
CBHW050024130526
44590CB00042B/1888